Speec
for You!

Third Edition

Elizabeth Sneddon

Professor Emeritus, University of Natal, Durban, South Africa

Edited and Revised by

Murray McGibbon

Department of Theatre and Drama, Indiana University, Bloomington, USA

KENDALL/HUNT PUBLISHING COMPANY

4050 Westmark Drive Dubuque, Iowa 52002

ISBN 0-7872-8202-2

Printed in the United States of America
10 9 8 7 6 5 4 3 2 1

Reading Maketh a Full Man:
Writing Maketh an Exact Man:
Speaking Maketh a Ready Man.

Francis Bacon

There's only one purpose in education, and that's to develop what a child has in him by giving information and understanding, so as to make him a living individual capable of enjoying himself as such, and of taking his proper place in a community. . . .

Teach him his own language in such a way that he will learn the spirit of it; not only because words are the principal condition of social life, but for this reason: whenever a man makes one of those lonely journeys into his own mind, or the secret places of his will, he takes with him, like a lamp to explore them, his native language. And so if he is to see anything it must be bright and strong. Language, among other things, is an instrument of the senses. Your finger tips are blunt, and your eyes are a blear, and your tongue's a flap of dead rubber that can't taste anything unless you have words to translate what they feel and see and relish, to your understanding.

Eric Linklater

Introduction

On a return visit to South Africa in 1999, I paid a visit to Elizabeth Sneddon at her home in Durban. During the years she has been my inspirational mentor, advisor, colleague and friend. At the time she enquired about my teaching experiences in the United States and I told her that one of my most useful teaching texts was *Speech Training for You* which I had first encountered as a drama student at the University of Natal in Pietermaritzburg in 1975. "Why don't you revise the text and get it published in America?" she quipped. The book you are now holding is the result of that brief encounter. Try as you read it to get a sense of Elizabeth Sneddon's passion, and that special ingredient that makes her an inspirational teacher—her humanity and insight into the human condition. No one who meets her can come away without learning more about the art of living and her absolute conviction that speech is man's greatest gift. She is a truly exceptional human being and it is a great pleasure to introduce her book to an American audience.

This book is intended for students who want to learn how to speak better and use their voices more effectively. It will be as useful to high school students as it will be to college students and beginning actors. In it you will find great poetry and literature with helpful hints on how to make language come alive. The third edition includes basic phonemic classification for the more advanced student, as well as revised phonetic symbols suggested by the International Phonetic Association (IPA).

It has been my experience teaching acting in the United States that many students fail to recognize what Aristotle knew—that acting is the correct manipulation of the voice to indicate character on stage. While there have been many acting texts published in recent years, none that I have encountered gives a rigorous and thorough training of the voice. Of course no book can teach you how to speak, but the lessons herein, regularly applied with discipline and care will help anyone willing to learn, become a better actor, speaker and communicator.

Murray McGibbon
Indiana University,
Bloomington, USA
August 2001

Contents

Preface

This book is written for everyone who realizes the importance of speech in the development of the human mind, and who wishes to improve his control of this medium of communication, whether he be a high school or college student, teacher or parent.

You can only judge if you know. This book aims at letting you *know* what you should *know* about speech.

This is not a book for the specialist. While the third edition includes phonemic classification terms, the book aims at:

- Explaining the facts in very clear and simple language.
- Providing a semester's work for those who want to undertake what is perhaps the most important aspect of education, as it certainly is the most neglected.

One of the problems of writing such a book, is that the theory is less important than the practice. You cannot learn to speak well by reading a text book, any more than you can become healthy by reading a medical book.

In this book you are shown how to set about training yourself to speak well. This is essentially a practical book. It tells you step by step what to do. It is arranged so that you will have plenty of material for practice, and so that, as you practice, you will begin to understand the immensely important connection between speech and literature. For this reason excerpts have been taken from great literature—for a correct and intelligent training in speech is a training in literary appreciation. A good speech teacher will know better than to listen to those who say "great literature" is spoilt by being used as material for practice. Nothing can spoil it. The chances are that in the end, with a deepened awareness borne of a quickened perception, the student who has used this practice material will make the effort to read more of what these authors have written, and so enter into his inheritance of one of the Realms of Gold!

As a teacher of speech, I have found clever nonsense rhymes invaluable for fixing a student's attention on the qualities of speech sounds, and very luckily I have found someone who signs herself "D.L." and who has a greater gift in this direction than anyone I know. I am indebted to Delphine Lethbridge for permission to use, for the purposes of this book, her most entertaining rhymes, as well as for encouragement and useful criticism.

There are many people who are really responsible for the existence of this book, and among them I must mention especially Mr. N. Nuttall, Miss M. Clark and Miss M. Martin, all of whom have urged me to undertake the task of publishing it. To them my thanks are due, as well as to Mrs. P. Robertson for her comments on the text.

To those who use this book, I can only say that I hope it fulfils its purpose. The strange thing about undertaking a course of speech training is that you will probably enjoy the experience enormously, for though you do not realize it at first, you are setting out on a voyage of discovery. At first you will discover many things about yourself, but as you progress you will find that your interest is becoming concentrated on a world forever widening on your view, and that is the joy of life—the endless quest!

Elizabeth Sneddon
Durban, South Africa

Acknowledgements from *Speech Training for You* by Elizabeth Sneddon, first published 1950.

ACKNOWLEDGMENT

The author and the publishers desire to record their grateful thanks to the following publishers and to the authors from whose works selections have been taken, for their generous permission to include certain poems, or extracts from poems, in this volume.

MESSRS. ALLEN & UNWIN LTD. for their kind permission to use a short extract from Gilbert Murray's translation of Aristophanes' *'The Frogs'*. Also to the translator, Mr. Gilbert Murray, for granting the right to reprint the few lines reprinted.

MESSRS. BURNS OATES & WASHBURN LTD. for permission to reprint the poem *'In No Strange Land,'* by Francis Thompson. Also to Sir Francis Meynell, the owner of the copyright, for his kind permission to republish the poem.

MESSRS. JONATHAN CAPE LTD. and MRS. W. H. DAVIES for *'The Kingfisher'* and *'The Rain'*, from *'The Collected Poems of W. H. Davies'*.

MESSRS. JONATHAN CAPE LTD. and the author for *'Portrait of a Machine'* from *'Roast Leviathan'* by Louis Untermeyer.

MESSRS. JONATHAN CAPE LTD. and the Executors of Herbert Trench for *'O Dreamy, Gloomy, Friendly Trees'* from *'The Collected Works of Herbert Trench'*, Vol. II.

MESSRS. THE CLARENDON PRESS for permission to use *'A Passer By'* from Robert Bridges' *'Shorter Poems'* by permission of the holders of the copyright, The Clarendon Press, Oxford.

MR. PEDRAIC COLUM for permission to reprint his poem, *'The Old Woman of the Road'*.

MRS. FRANCES M. CORNFORD for her kind permission to include her poem, *'Grand Ballet'*.

MESSRS. GERALD DUCKWORTH LTD. for permission to reprint *'Tarantella'*, by Hilaire Belloc. Our thanks are also made to Mr. Belloc for his kind permission.

MESSRS. FABER & FABER LTD., MR. WALTER DE LA MARE and MISS U. F. BARTON for permission to use the following four poems by Mr. de la Mare, *'Sam'*, *'The Listeners'*, *'Tartary'*, and *'Tewkesbury Road'*.

For permission to reprint the poem *'I Think Continually of Those'*, by Stephen Spender, taken from the volume of *'Poems'* by Stephen Spender. Our grateful acknowledgment and thanks are also made to the author.

MESSRS. GEO. G. HARRAP & CO. LTD. for permission to use the poem, *'The Ballad of Semmerwater'*, by the late Sir William Watson, taken from *'The Poems of Sir William Watson, 1878–1935'*.

Chapter 1

The Spoken Word

Speech training is the most important of all aspects of education. Without speech no other study is possible, for speech is the chief instrument of communication and self-development of all human beings.

There is widespread ignorance of speech work and its implications. Consequently it is the most neglected of all studies. Because we can all speak after a fashion we tend to lose sight of the tremendous importance of this study, yet speech lies at the basis of all civilization. "Speech is to thought what protoplasm is to life." The study of the progress of a race in civilization is mirrored in its control of the spoken word, and no less is the progress of the individual human mind mirrored in that control.

Make no mistake about this. Reading and writing are merely mechanical ways of recording speech. In the beginning was the *spoken word,* and that spoken word was the life of the mind.

Have you ever paused to consider all that is involved in speaking a word? A word has three aspects—a physical, an intellectual and an emotional aspect. Any successful process of speech training must take into account all three aspects of speech. The neglect of any one of these aspects can lead only to a warped and imperfect training, which will manifest itself in all sorts of absurdities, while a discipline in all three aspects will involve a discipline of the whole personality.

Therefore, whatever study we neglect, we cannot afford to neglect the study of our own language in order to gain as complete a control of it as possible, for in doing so, we are called upon to exercise all aspects of our being—including the physical, the mental, and the emotional aspects.

Frequently, I am asked, "What is the test of good speech?" If I have to reply briefly, the answer is: "Speech which is free from strain, including physical strain, mental strain, and emotional strain."

Perhaps the final test of good speech is that it conveys to the listener, without attracting attention to itself, what the speaker intended to convey—neither more nor less.

On the physical level, speech attracts attention to itself when it is high-pitched, harsh, thin, difficult to hear or indistinct. These are all defects of speech which are due to a failure to understand and control the physical processes of speech. This failure can sometimes have very disastrous consequences, which range from lack of success in earning a living to a nervous breakdown in the attempt to do so.

There is no normal human being who cannot eliminate every speech defect which may at present be a handicap to him. But speech training cannot be done in "a cram course", nor can it be achieved merely by reading a book. The theory and practice of speech training cannot be satisfactorily separated. You must first know, and then apply, your knowledge daily, until, through practice, you achieve a mastery that enables you to speak without thinking how you breathe, or how you shape your speech sounds.

The Physical Aspects of Speech

In order to master the physical aspects of speech you must concentrate on *five* points:

1. Learn to relax.
2. Improve your breath control.
3. Develop resonance.
4. Shape the vowel sounds correctly.
5. Gain a flexible control of the articulative organs in shaping the consonant sounds.

CHAPTER 2

Relaxation

Since every tension in the body is registered in the voice, and consequently communicated to the listener, it is important that the speaker should be trained to relax, and this can be done by practicing a few very simple exercises.

Stand in a well-balanced position, with feet slightly apart, chest up, shoulders down and chin in. Do the following exercises for relaxing:

1. *The Windmill Exercise*
   Allow the arms to hang loosely at the sides. From that position—
   a. Rotate, from the shoulder, the right arm twenty times in an *anti-clockwise* direction.
   b. Repeat this exercise with the left arm.
   c. Repeat this exercise rotating both arms at the same time. Allow the arms to swing freely. Do not force them round.
2. *Head Rotating Exercise*
   a. Practice allowing the head to rotate first in a clockwise and then in an anti-clockwise direction.
   b. Repeat this exercise ten times in each direction.
   c. Once again, remember not to use force. Let the weight of the head determine the rotation.
3. *Waist Rotating Exercise*
   Practice rotating the upper part of the body from the waist in a clockwise direction ten times, and then repeat the movement in an anti-clockwise direction.
4. *Leg Swinging Exercise*
   a. Stand on the left leg. Preserve your balance by holding on to the back of a chair with your left hand. Swing the right leg forward and then back as far as it will go.
   b. Repeat this movement rhythmically twenty times. Then stand on your right leg holding the chair with your right hand and repeat the exercise, this time swinging the left leg.
5. *Toe Touching Exercise*
   a. Raise the arms above the head, then bend forward from the waist to touch the toes with the finger tips. Repeat the movement touching the right toes with the left hand, and then the left toes with the right hand.
      Do these movements rhythmically.

b. Resume the balanced stance which you had when you began the exercises, and you will find that you are in a good state to begin your breathing exercises. When you stand, sit, or lie down, see that your body is free from strain.

How to Stand

Stand in a balanced position, with the feet slightly apart, the weight on the forward foot, the shoulders back and down, the chest raised, and the chin in.

How to Sit

Sit well back in your chair, supporting the base of the spine against the chair back. Place the weight—not on the end of the spine—but on the thighs. See that the elbows are at their natural level, so that the shoulders are not hunched. Keep your shoulders down. Keep the chest raised. Keep the hands and feet quite still. Do not cross the knees, as this interferes with the circulation of the blood, and must inevitably set up tensions in the body.

CHAPTER 3

Breath Control

Voice is vibrating breath, so it follows that if you are to be audible, and that is your first duty as a speaker, you must have:

a. A sufficient volume of breath.
b. A good control of it.

How to Improve the Volume of Breath

a. Stand in a well-balanced, relaxed position.
b. Breathe through the nose and allow the breath to fill the lungs evenly.

Since the lungs—two sponge-like masses of air cells—fill the chest cavity, except for the space occupied by the heart, the chest must expand as you breathe in.

If you are breathing correctly the chest will expand in three directions:

i. The ribs will move out. The greatest expansion will be in the lower ribs.
ii. The breast bone will swing up and out, so that the space between the spine and the breast bone will be increased.
iii. The diaphragm, which is a dome-shaped muscle forming the floor of the chest and the roof of the abdominal cavity, will move into a plate-like position as the lungs fill.

Do not allow the abdominal wall to bulge as you breathe in, but on the other hand do not contract the abdominal wall until you begin to breathe out.

How to Breathe Out

Keep your shoulders down and the upper part of your chest raised. Allow the abdominal wall to contract very slowly, so that the diaphragm moves back slowly, and without any jerking, into its dome-shaped position. Hold your ribs lightly out, as long as you can. Replenish your breath supply before the upper chest collapses.

Your breath should be expelled from the base of the lungs. As a speaker your aim is to maintain an unbroken column of breath between the base of the lungs and the lips, so it is very important that you should learn to control the outgoing breath. The majority of people make the mistake of expelling the breath first from the upper part of the lungs. This causes the upper chest to collapse, and destroys the control of the outgoing breath on which the quality of your voice depends.

Daily Exercises for Improving Volume and Breath Control

Each exercise must be done five times. Remember to stand in a relaxed and well-balanced position.

1. a. Breathe in through the nose, filling the lungs evenly and expanding the chest in three directions. Do not grow rigid or allow any strain to develop. Hold the breath while you silently count up to ten.

   Breathe out slowly through the nose, keeping the upper chest expanded and allowing the abdominal wall slowly to contract.

   b. Repeat exercise 1(a) breathing in through the nose and out through the mouth, thus:

   BREATHE IN, two, three, four, five, six, seven, eight.
   HOLD, two, three.
   OUT, two, three, four, five, six, seven, eight.

   Repeat this exercise ten times.

   c. Repeat the exercise breathing in through the mouth and out through the mouth.

   d. Repeat the exercise, breathing in through the mouth and out through the nose.

   N.B.—All breathing exercises should be done rhythmically.

2. Breathe in, allow the lower jaw to relax completely till there is a space of at least an inch and a half between the upper and lower teeth.

   Intone the sound *"Ah"* until the outgoing breath is completely expelled.

   Remember to use the abdominal press, emptying the lungs from the base, and so maintaining a steadily vibrating column of breath.

3. Breathe in, and count aloud using all the breath to say the sound *"One"*.

   Repeat, using half the breath to say *"One"* and half to say *"Two"*. Repeat this exercise, adding one more number each time until you are able to count up to *twenty-four* in one breath, giving a full, rounded tone to each sound.

   At first you will not be able to count beyond eight or nine in a full, rounded tone, but practicing every day for a semester will enable you to reach twenty-four easily.

   It is possible to devise many variations of these basic breathing exercises, but it is important to remember all the time that you are aiming at improving your control of an increased volume of breath.

Do not use force in your effort to increase your volume or control. Do not overtire yourself or prolong the exercises beyond the point at which you enjoy yourself.

In all your exercises remember that the exercise of will-power, without understanding, will defeat the end you have in view. To strain yourself or to *force* yourself to achieve a goal is to be defeated before you begin. The right way to do a thing is the only successful way. Learn to understand, and don't be too hard on yourself.

CHAPTER 4

Resonance

A voice that lacks resonance remains thin and reed-like. This seriously impairs the flexibility of a voice, and means that it can neither convey the speaker's meaning adequately, nor hold the attention of the listener. Nothing is more boring than a monotonous voice. Lack of resonance is a voice defect which can be remedied by conscientiously practicing exercises which will increase resonance.

Voice is vibrating breath, so obviously breath control is a preliminary to achieving resonance. Practice breathing exercises to increase the volume of the breath before you begin on Resonance Exercises. In fact, do your breathing exercises every day.

A resonator is a cavity in which sound can be reinforced, expanded, made greater. A voice is a tiny squeak until it is expanded in the head resonators. There are resonators in the chest, the throat and the head.

The head resonators are the resonators on which to concentrate. Perhaps the most simple approach is to learn how to use the mouth as a resonator.

Learn to Relax the Lower Jaw

1. Sit in a chair and rest the right elbow on a table, holding the forearm up. Then allow the hand to fall by its own weight. As the hand drops allow the jaw to drop in a perfectly relaxed way.

   I shall refer to this as the Yogi exercise.

   Repeat this exercise at least twenty times. Do not force the lower jaw. Allow it to drop. There should be a space of at least an inch and a half between the upper and lower teeth, when the lower jaw is allowed to drop.
2. Intone the word "*Down*" twenty times. Concentrate on achieving a perfectly relaxed lower jaw as you shape the vowel sound.

How to Intone

In saying the vowel sound of each syllable, drop the lower jaw as much as possible, and expend a great deal of vibrating breath in prolonging, i.e., lengthening, the vowel sound. *Each syllable should be of equal length* when you are intoning.

Resonance Exercises

1. Place the lips lightly together, but keep the upper and lower teeth apart, then hum, taking care to press the breath out of the lungs by using the abdominal press and consciously filling the mouth with breath, so that the vibrating breath causes a sensation of tickling on the lips. Continue to hum until the breath is exhausted, and then repeat this exercise ten times.
2. Repeat this humming exercise, but in order to improve the forward placing of the voice on the lips, preface the humming sound with a sound shaped on the lips.

   B............. mmmmmmmmmm
   P............. mmmmmmmmmm
   W............ mmmmmmmmmm, etc.

3. Intone on long vowel sounds, such as "Ah". Prolong the following sounds until the breath is exhausted, then take another breath and repeat.

Ah....................	Oh...................
Aw....................	Oo...................
Ow..................	

   Repeat this intoning exercise using the following words:

Mah	Maw	Mow	Moh	Mooo
Lah	Law	Low	Loh	Looo
Wah	Waw	Wow	Woh	Wooo

Exercises for Developing the Use of the Throat as a Resonator

a. Practice yawning. This is the best possible exercise for expanding the throat. To yawn, drop the lower jaw and breathe in through the mouth.
b. Intone:

   Ah......... Aw......... Ow........ Ooo.......

Exercises for Developing Nasal Resonance

a. Practice humming until you can feel the vibration on the top of your head.
b. Make lists of words with "M" as the initial sound, and intone on the initial sound.

March	Murmur	Moist
Marvel	Marble	Mavis

c. Make lists of words with the initial "N" sound, and intone this sound as you utter the word.

Not	Never	Gnat	Gnarl	No

d. Make lists of words ending in "ng" and practice holding this sound.

King	Singing	Leaping
Ring	Winging	Sweeping
Swing	Bringing	Hurling

Fling	Ringing	Reaping
Sing	Flinging	Screaming

e. Verses on which to practice intoning to improve resonance:

Ode:

We are the music-makers,
And we are dreamers of dreams,
Wandering by lone sea-breakers,
And sitting by desolate streams;—
World-losers and world-forsakers,
On whom the pale moon gleams:
Yet we are the movers and shakers
Of the world for ever, it seems.
With wonderful deathless ditties
We build up the world's great cities,
And out of a fabulous story
We fashion an empire's glory:
One man with a dream, at pleasure,
Shall go forth and conquer a crown;
And three with a new song's measure
Can trample a kingdom down.
We, in the ages lying
In the buried past of the earth,
Built Nineveh with our sighing,
And Babel itself in our mirth;
And overthrew them with prophesying
To the old of the new world's worth;
For each age is a dream that is dying,
Or one that is coming to birth.
A breath of our inspiration
Is the life of each generation;
A wondrous thing of our dreaming,
Unearthly, impossible seeming—
The soldier, the king, and the peasant
Are working together as one,
Till our dream shall become their present,
And their work in the world be done.
—Arthur W. O'Shaughnessey.

How to Use the Above Verse for Practice in Resonance

Intone the following groups of vowels:

ee	ah	oo	ay (As in make).
[i]	[a]	[u]	[eɪ] (Phonetic symbols).

Repeat this *three* times:

ee	ah	oo	ay
ee	ah	oo	ay
ee	ah	oo	ay

The above vowel sounds are to be found in the first phrase of the poem.

Now intone the words of the first phrase: "We are the music makers."

Concentrate on lengthening the vowel sounds.

Intone three times.

Then *say*, "We are the music makers". Notice how your lower jaw opens on every syllable. That is what it should be doing in ordinary speech.

Think now, not of the sound of the phrase, but of the meaning, and repeat the phrase.

We are the music makers

Do you notice how, in order to make the meaning clear, you vary the pace at which you utter the words?

When you intone, the pace is even and the same amount of breath is used on each syllable, but when you say it to convey the meaning, you pause after "we" and then you stress "music" and "makers", because those are the words that are the most important in that phrase.

Remember *intoning* is only useful for increasing breath control and resonance. It is *not* a way of speaking. In speaking, the meaning matters most; all the other aspects of speech should be so right that we take no notice of them when speaking.

Intoning is to the speaker what scales are to the pianist, a way of increasing technical control.

Now let us go back to "The Music Makers".

Pick out *all* the *long* vowels in each phrase.

Write them down.

Intone them *three* times.

Then intone the complete phrase, training yourself to listen so that you know whether you are giving the vowels their due length. Then say the phrase for the meaning.

After you have worked on each phrase intone the vowels of the whole verse.

a. Then intone the whole verse.
b. Then say the whole verse.

Ultimately you will have practiced this extract so often that you will know the verses by heart.

4. Intone any passage of verse or prose three times and then say it opening the mouth well and using the same breath control, but concentrating entirely on the meaning of the passage.

Passages containing many long vowels and the following consonants L, M, N, NG and R, will furnish the best material for practice. The two passages given below will afford further practice in intoning:

Extract From the Tragical History of Doctor Faustus

Ah, Faustus,
Now hast thou but one bare hour to live,
And then thou must be damned perpetually!
Stand still, you ever moving spheres of Heaven,
That time may cease and midnight never come;
Fair Nature's eye, rise, rise again and make
Perpetual day; or let this hour be but
A year, a month, a week, a natural day,
That Faustus may repent and save his soul!
O lente, lente currite noctis equi!
The stars move still, time runs, the clock will strike,
The Devil will come, and Faustus must be damned.
O I'll leap up to my God! Who pulls me down?
See, see where Christ's blood streams in the firmament!
One drop would save my soul—half a drop! ah, my Christ!
Ah, rend not my heart for naming of my Christ!
Yet will I call on Him!—O spare me, Lucifer!—
Where is it now? 'Tis gone; and see where God
Stretcheth out his arm, and bends his ireful brows!—
Mountain and hills, come, come and fall on me,
And hide me from the heavy wrath of God!

—Christopher Marlowe.

Now say the above passage concentrating on the meaning.

Selection from Letter V

In China, letters are respected not merely to a degree, but in a sense which must seem, I think to Western minds, unintelligible and overstrained. But there is a reason for it. Our poets and literary men have taught their successors for long generations to look for good not in wealth, not in power, not in miscellaneous activity, but in a trained, a choice, an exquisite appreciation of the most simple and universal relations of life. To feel, and in order to feel, to express (or at least to understand the expression of) all that is lovely in Nature, all that is poignant and sensitive in man, is, to us, in itself a sufficient end.

A rose in a moonlit garden, the shadow of trees on turf, almond bloom, scent of pine; the wine cup and the guitar; these, and the pathos of life and death, the long embrace, the hand stretched out in vain, the moment that glides for ever away with its freight of music and light, into the shadow and the hush of the haunted past. All that we have; all that eludes us: a bird on the wind, a perfume escaped on the gale—to all these things we are trained to respond, and the response is what we call literature. This we have. This you cannot give us; but this you may so easily take away. Amid the roar of looms it cannot be heard; it cannot be seen in the smoke of factories; it is killed by the wear and the whirl of Western life. And when I look at your business men, the men whom you most admire; when I see them hour after hour, day after day, year after year, toiling in the mill of their forced and undelighted labours . . . I reflect, I confess with satisfaction, on the simpler routine of our ancient industry, and prize above all your new and dangerous routes, the beaten track so familiar to our accustomed feet, that we have leisure, even while we pace it, to turn our gaze up to the eternal stars.

—*G. Lowes Dickinson.*

Now say the above passage concentrating on the meaning.

CHAPTER 5

Vowel Sounds

You can speak, but how well you speak depends largely on how you shape your vowel sounds.

There are two kinds of Speech Sounds. Vowel sounds and Consonant sounds.

The shaping of vowel sounds is called Enunciation.

The shaping of consonant sounds is called Articulation.

The carrying power of the voice is largely dependent on the way in which vowel sounds are shaped.

All vowel sounds are shaped in the oral cavity and come through a free opening of the mouth.

A preliminary to good shaping of vowel sounds is good breath control. The test of good vowel sounds is that they are free from strain. The most common mistake made by speakers in shaping vowel sounds is to shape them not in the mouth but in the throat, using the pharynx as an organ of speech, when it should be used as a resonator only.

The pharynx is the space between the back of the tongue and the back wall of the throat.

Exercise for expanding the pharynx: PRACTICE YAWNING.

Remember that the pharynx is a resonator. Do not attempt to use it, or any part of it, for the shaping of vowel sounds. If you do, your lower jaw will be rigid and your vowel sounds distorted.

The most important organs of speech used in shaping vowel sounds are the *tongue* and the *lips.*

The following are useful exercises for increasing the flexibility of the lips.

Repeat the following groups of sounds each ten times:

a.	Ee—oo	Ee—oo	Ee—oo
b.	Oo—w	Oo—w	Oo—w
c.	Ee—oo—w	Ee—oo—w	Ee—oo—w
d.	Bow—wow	Bow—wow	Bow—wow
e.	W—oo	W—oo	W—oo
f.	Oo—ee	Oo—ee	Oo—ee
g.	W—oo—ee	W—oo—ee	W—oo—ee
h.	Oo—w—ee	Oo—w—ee	Oo—w—ee

Exercises for Increasing the Flexibility of Your Tongue

1. The "North, South, East, West" Exercise.

   Put your tongue out as far as it will go and making it as pointed as possible—

   a. Turn it up towards your nose.
   b. Turn it down towards your chin.
   c. Stretch it to the dimple on your left cheek.
   d. Stretch it to the dimple on your right cheek.

   Repeat this operation *five* times.
2. Open your mouth well.

   Curl your tongue up towards the palate and, with the tongue tip, stroke the palate from the uvula to the front teeth. Repeat this exercise five times, and then place the tongue tip behind the upper teeth and move it across the palate towards the uvula.
3. Hold up the index finger of your right hand at a distance at which the tongue will have to be stretched for the tongue tip to reach it. Move the tongue tip up and down the index finger. Do not move the finger!

Rules for Improving Enunciation

1. Learn to listen to yourself. Learn to listen to yourself.
2. Relax! Relax! Relax!
3. Remember to shape all vowel sounds forward in the mouth, not on the pharynx.

Vowel Phonetic Symbols

This book lists twenty four vowel sounds, each of which is tabulated below along with the appropriate phonetic symbols.

1	AH	as in "father"	ɑ or a
2	AW	as in "bought"	ɔ
3	OO	as in "moon"	u
4	OW	as in "cow"	ɑʊ or au
5	OU	as in "blow"	oʊ or ou
6	A	as in "save"	eɪ
7	i	as in "sight"	aɪ or ai
8	e	as in "bed"	ɛ
9	a	as in "bat"	æ
10	I	as in "pit"	ɪ
11	OY	as in "boy"	ɔɪ or ɔi
12	u	as in "rub"	ʌ
13	U	as in "wool"	ʊ or U
14	A	as in "about"	ə
15	o	as in "not"	ɒ

16	EE	as in "need"	i
17	IR	as in "bird"	ɜ or ɝ
18	AIR	as in "pair"	ɛə or ɛɚ
19	EAR	as in "fear"	ɪə or ɪɚ or ir
20	OAR	as in "more"	ɔə or ɔɚ or ɔr
21	OOR	as in "poor"	ʊə or ʊɚ or ur
22	YEW	as in "few"	ju
23	URE	as in "pure"	jʊə or jʊɚ
24	IRE	as in "squire"	aɪə or aɪɚ

In the pages that follow practice will be given in each of the vowel sounds, arranged in the order in which they can be most satisfactorily dealt with from the point of view of learning to perceive their sound and shape.

How the Vowels are Shaped

1. "AH" [ɑ] as in "father"

ɑ

or

a

"AH"

Symbols: [ɑ] SCRIPT A or [a] LOWER CASE A

Phonemic classification: [ɑ] open back unrounded; [a] front unrounded

IPA usage: "father"; "hard"; "star"

American English usage: "park"; "spa"; "odd" (also pronounced [a] or [ɒ])

Allow the tongue to lie perfectly relaxed in the lower jaw with the tongue tip touching the lower teeth. Drop the lower jaw as far as it will go and intone on the "AH" sound, until the tidal breath is exhausted, remembering to use the abdominal press as you breathe out.

Consciously endeavor to fill the mouth with vibrating breath.

Repeat this exercise about ten times.

a. Practice saying the following rhyme, paying particular attention to the "AH" sound wherever it appears.

Martha found a marble,
and half a dozen jars
Of jade green flashes
plucked from the stars.
Martha found a farmer,
farming on his farm,
Martha plucked the farmer,
much to his alarm.

She jammed him in a jar,
with the marble and the star,
Then threw him far away—
and to this day—
(so people say)
A farmer gazes down from Mars,
Outshining all the brightest stars!
—D.L.

b. Make a list of fifty words containing the "AH" sound.

e.g.	Farm	Are	Heart
	Star	Marble	Harvest
	Hard	Market	Hardship
	Car		

Practice saying these words, giving full value to the "AH" sound. A useful preliminary exercise is to intone each word. Then say the word using the *same volume of breath and dropping the lower jaw* just as far as when you intoned it, but concentrating now on the meaning of the word, visualizing the idea.

See in your mind's eye the picture that the word conjures up. At the same time listen to the sounds.

c. Make up a number of verses, using words containing this sound. As you search for words, and as you repeat the verses, you will grow conscious of the sound.
d. Practice saying the sound in the throat and then forward in the mouth. Notice how the throat and lower jaw tighten when the sound is shaped in the throat, and how harsh it is. Then notice how full-toned, musical and pleasant it is when it is shaped forward in the mouth with the lower jaw completely relaxed.
e. Memorize the following poem which has been chosen because of the number of words which contain the "AH" sound. From the point of view of speech training, it is useless to memorize silently. You must say the extract aloud so often that ultimately you know it by heart. Try to speak it as you imagine it would have been spoken by such people as the Pilgrims, the merchants and the watchman. Do not shout. Use a full-toned, low-pitched voice, but get the power in it by good breath control, not by brute force.

Selection From "The Golden Journey to Samarkand"

THE PILGRIMS:

We are the Pilgrims, master; we shall go
Always a little farther: it may be
Beyond that last blue mountain barred with snow,
Across that angry or that glimmering sea,
White on a throne or guarded in a cave
There lives a prophet who can understand
Why men were born: but surely we are brave,
Who make the Golden Journey to Samarkand.

The Chief Merchant:
We gnaw the nail of hurry. Master, away!

One of the Women:
O turn your eyes to where your children stand.
Is not Baghdad the beautiful? O stay!

The Merchants:
We take the Golden Road to Samarkand.

An Old Man:
Have not you girls and garlands in your homes,
Eunuchs and Syrian boys at your command?
Seek not excess; God hateth him who roams!

The Merchants:
We make the Golden Journey to Samarkand.

A Pilgrim with a Beautiful Voice:
Sweet to ride forth at evening from the wells
When shadows pass gigantic on the sand,
And softly through the silence beat the bells
Along the Golden Road to Samarkand.

A Merchant:
We travel not for trafficking alone;
By hotter winds our fiery hearts are fanned:
For lust of knowing what should not be known
We make the Golden Journey to Samarkand.

The Master of the Caravan:
Open the gate, O watchman of the night!

The Watchman:
Ho, travellers, I open. For what land
Leave you the dim-moon city of delight?

The Merchants (with a shout):
We make the Golden Journey to Samarkand.
(The caravan passes through the Gate).

The Watchman (consoling the women):
What would ye, ladies? It was ever thus.
Men are unwise and curiously planned.

A Woman:
They have their dreams, and do not think of us.

Voices of the Caravan (in the distance, singing):
We make the Golden Journey to Samarkand.

—James Elroy Flecker.

2. "AW" [ɔ] as in "bought"

ɔ

BROAD "AW"

Symbol: OPEN O

Phonemic classification: open mid back rounded

IPA usage: "bought"; "yawn"; "ball"

American English usage: "bought"; "wall" (also pronounced as [ɒ] or [ɑ])

Drop the lower jaw as far as you did for the "AH" sound, and then purse the lips slightly without raising the lower jaw. Allow the base of the tongue to rise slightly towards the soft palate. Intone the sound "AW".

Repeat ten times.

a. Say the following verse, paying particular attention to the "AW" sound in the words in which it occurs.

Dawn was a prawn who lived in the sea,
Dawn was naughty, as naughty could be.
Her mother despaired of her little daughter—
Her father felt sad, for he always had taught her.
To be a good prawn,
From the day she was born.

Then Dawn was caught,
She was caught in a net.
She was boiled in a basin,
And then she was set
In a jelly, and made into tastiest brawn,
What a really unfortunate death
for a prawn!

—D.L.

Remember to fill the lungs and use the abdominal press in expelling the breath which you shape into words.

b. Intone the following words:

Maul	Yawn	Tall	Fawn
Stall	Prawn	Fall	Lawn
Hall	Sawn	Ball	Dawn

Then say these words, paying particular attention to the length of the vowel sound.

c. Make a list of fifty words containing this sound.

d. Memorize the following poem, which means say it aloud seventy-seven times!

It has been chosen because it will afford you, among other things, an opportunity to practice "AW" sounds.

Grand Ballet

I saw you dance that summer before the war.
One thunderous night it was, at Covent Garden,
When we, who walked, beneath the weighted tree,
Hot metropolitan pavements, might have smelt
Blood in the dust, and heard the traffic's cry
Ceaseless, and savage, like a prophecy.

As by a sunrise sea I saw you stand,
Your sylphides round you on the timeless strand
White, pure, delicious poised butterflies,
The early nineteenth century in their eyes,
And Chopin ready for their silver toes.
(O sighs unsatisfied, and one red rose!).
The fountain of all movement ready to flow
Seemed prisoned in your entranced body. So
You stood, their Prince, most elegantly fair,
Swan-sleeved, black-jacketed, with falling hair
And hands half-raised in ravishment. O there,
You Grecian arrow, fitted to the bow,
You beech tree in a legendary wood,
You panther in a velvet bolero,
There you for one immortal moment stood.

One moment like a wave before it flows,
Frozen in perfectness. Then one hand rose
And tossed a silver curl, demurely light.
(O grace, O rose, O Chopin and all delight),
And the enchantment broke!
That thunderous night
We saw Nijinsky dance.
Thereafter fell
On the awaiting world the powers of Hell,
Chaos, and irremediable pain;
And utter darkness on your empty brain,
Not even grief to say, No more, no more.

But tell me, when my mortal memories wane,
As death draws near, and peace is mine and pardon,
Where will it like an escaped dove repair?
To what Platonic happy Heaven—where?—O where?

Untouchable by fate and free of Time,
That one immortal moment of the mime
We saw Nijinsky dance at Covent Garden?
—*Frances Cornford.*

3. "OO" [u] as in "moon"

u

LONG "OO"

Symbol: LOWER-CASE U
Phonemic classification: close back rounded
IPA usage: "moon"; "spoon"; "juice"
American English usage: same as IPA

Put your thumb in your mouth. Draw the lips up round it. Remove your thumb, keeping the lips in that rounded and protruding position. Intone the sound "OO" while maintaining this lip position.

Remember that you must empty your lungs from the base. Try to prolong this sound. It should sound like the wind sighing, or a cow mooing.

a. Say the following verse, paying particular attention to the "OO" sound in the words in which it occurs.

The dove said—"Coo,
How do you do?
It's nice to see you, Mr. Sun,
It's nice to see you,
Though it's true
You've come to tell me day's begun.
I'm very glad that night is through,
Because I've got so much to do.
A nest to furnish,
and it's so
Hard to buy a twig you know.
I rather fancy something blue,
Perhaps a blue gum twig will do.
But I must fly, to peck some food—
So please don't think I'm very rude,
When I pray, don't fade too soon
To make a way for Mr. Moon!"
—*D.L.*

b. Intone the following words and then say them, paying particular attention to the length of the vowel sound:

Boom	Moon	Pool
Room	Broom	Ruler
Loom	Croon	Rude
Tomb	Coon	Cool
Doom	Spoon	School

c. Make a list of fifty words containing the "OO" sound.

d. Pay attention to the way in which you say these words. Do not try to say the sound before your lips are in the correct position.

e. Speak the following verses which have been specially chosen to afford you practice in shaping the "OO" sound:

The Night Wind

Have you ever heard the wind go, "Yoooooo"?
Tis a pitiful sound to hear!
It seems to chill you through and through
With a strange and speechless fear.
'Tis the voice of the night that broods outside
When folks should be asleep,
And many and many's the time I've cried
To the darkness brooding far and wide
Over the land and the deep:
"Whom do you want, O lonely night
That you wail the long hours through?"
And the night would say in its ghostly way:
"Yoooooooo!
Yoooooooo!
Yoooooooo!"

My mother told me long ago
(When I was a little lad)
That when the night went wailing so,
Somebody had been bad;
And then, when I was snug in bed,
Whither I had been sent,
With the blankets pulled up round my head,
I'd think of what my mother'd said,
And wonder what boy she meant!
And "who's been bad today?" I'd ask
Of the wind that hoarsely blew,
And the voice would say in its meaningful way:
"Yoooooooo!
Yoooooooo!
Yoooooooo!"

That this was true I must allow—
You'll not believe it, though!
Yes, though I'm quite a model now,
I was not always so,
And if you doubt the things I say
Suppose you make the test;
Suppose, when you've been bad some day
And up to bed are sent away
From mother and the rest—
Suppose you ask, "Who has been bad?"
And then you'll hear what's true;
For the wind will moan in its ruefullest tone:
"Yoooooooo!
Yoooooooo!
Yoooooooo!"

—Eugene Field.

Underline the "OO" sounds in the last two verses.

Say the "YOOOO" in imitation of the wind as it reaches a crescendo and then fades out.

f. Memorize the following extract. Try to visualize the picture.

The Albatross

Stretching white wings in strenuous repose,
Sleeving them in the silver frills of sleep,
As I was carried, far from other foes,
To shear the long horizons of the deep,

A swift ship struck me down: through gusty glooms
I spun from fierce collision with her spars:
Shrill through the sleety pallor of my plumes
Whistled the golden bullets of the stars:

Loose on the gale my shattered wreck was strewn
And, conquered by the envious winds at last,
A rag upon the red horns of the moon,
Was tossed and gored and trampled by the blast.

Flapping the water like a sodden flag,
No more to rise, shot down by stormy guns,
How shamefully these great sprained sinews drag
That bracketed my purpose with the sun's. . . .

—Roy Campbell.

g. From the above extract select all the words which have the "OO" sound and practice these, e.g., through, gloomy, plumes. Learn to listen to the length of this sound and increase its vocality.

4. "OW" [aʊ] as in "cow."

aʊ

or

au

"AH OO"

Symbols: LOWER-CASE A/UPSILON

Phonemic Classification: Low-central Lax unrounded to high-back tense rounded

IPA usage: "cow"; "crown"

American English usage: "ouch"; "power"; "house"

Drop your lower jaw.

Remember that this time you are not saying one vowel sound but two. The second vowel sound is produced when the lower jaw begins to move up after it has been lowered to shape the previous vowel sound.

As a preliminary to saying this sound, intone:

Ah—oo	Ah—oo	Ah—oo—ow
Mah—oo	Mah—oo	Mah—oo—m*ow*
Nah—oo	Nah—oo	Nah—oo—n*ow*
Lah—oo	Lah—oo	Lah—oo—l*ow*

This will give you some idea of the movement of the lower jaw which is relaxed and the lips are apart. The front of the tongue is slightly tensed. From this position the base of the tongue is raised towards the soft palate and advanced very slightly. Take time to distinguish the two movements a + ʊ, and then practice gliding one into the other. Notice that the lips move from a neutral to a rounded position.

a. Now practice the following verses, paying particular attention to the shaping of the frequently occurring "OW" sounds in the words:

I heard a sound,
Below the ground,
A melancholy,
hollow sound.

I turned around,
I looked around,
I followed carefully
the sound:

Until I found,
Way down, down,
down,

A ditch,
A witch,
Who scowled and howled.

I never asked her why she did—
I thought it better if I hid!
—D.L.

b. Intone the following words and then say them, paying particular attention to the length of the vowel sounds:

Cow	Out	Brown	Sound
Now	Rout	Town	Pound
How	About	Crown	Ground
Plough	Stout	Frown	Round
Bough	Scout	Down	Found

c. Make a list of fifty words containing the "OW" sound.
d. Pay attention to the way in which you say these words. Do not try to say the sound before your lips are in the correct position.
e. The following two poems have been selected for practice because they contain a number of words which have the vowel sound "aʊ".

They have other features worth considering as well. For instance, how do they differ from each other? What are they about?

The Daffodils

I wandered lonely as a cloud
That floats on high o'er vales and hills,
When all at once I saw a crowd,
A host of golden daffodils;
Beside the lake, beneath the trees,
Fluttering and dancing in the breeze.

Continuous as the stars that shine
And twinkle on the Milky Way
They stretched in never-ending line
Along the margin of a bay:
Ten thousand saw I at a glance,
Tossing their heads in sprightly dance.

The waves beside them danced; but they
Out-did the sparkling waves in glee:

A poet could not but be gay,
In such a jocund company:
I gazed—and gazed—but little thought
What wealth the show to me had brought:

For oft, when on my couch I lie
In vacant or in pensive mood,
They flash upon that inward eye
Which is the bliss of solitude;
And then my heart with pleasure fills,
And dances with the daffodils.
—W. Wordsworth.

The Voice of the Lobster

'Tis the voice of the Lobster; I heard him declare,
"You have baked me too brown, I must sugar my hair,"
As a duck with its eyelids, so he with his nose
Trims his belt and his buttons, and turns out his toes.
When the sands are all dry, he is gay as a lark,
And will talk in contemptuous tones of the Shark:
But, when the tide rises and sharks are around,
His voice has a timid and tremulous sound.

I passed by his garden, and marked, with one eye,
How the Owl and the Panther were sharing a pie:
The Panther took pie-crust, and gravy, and meat,
While the Owl had the dish as its share of the treat.
When the pie was all finished, the Owl, as a boon,
Was kindly permitted to pocket the spoon:
While the Panther received knife and fork with a growl,
And concluded the banquet—
—Lewis Carroll.

5. "O" [oʊ] as in "blow"

oʊ

or

o

LONG "O"

Symbols: LOWER-CASE O/UPSILON or LOWER CASE O

Phonemic Classification: Close mid-back rounded

IPA usage: "blow"; float"; "rope"

American English usage: "grow"; "woe"; "note"

Open your mouth so that the space between your upper and lower teeth is about one inch. Round your lips and then intone "O". See how long you can hold this sound.

A good test of lip rounding is to draw your lips round the base of your thumb. Then remove your thumb while maintaining this lip rounding.

a. Now practice the following verse, paying particular attention to the shaping of the frequently occurring "O" sounds in the words:

Jeremy's pony
is big and bony,
Christopher's pony
Is fat.
So isn't it lucky
that Christopher's bony
And
Jeremy's short and fat!
If two were bony,
Owner and Pony,
Or
Two of them were fat,
They'd look like poles,
or plump sausage rolls,
How dreadful to contemplate that!

—D.L.

b. Intone the following words and then say them, paying particular attention to the length of the vowel sound:

Hold	Mole	Boat	Soap
Mould	Pole	Coat	Pope
Cold	Sole	Float	Hope
Rolled	Foal	Goat	Rope
Sold	Goal	Wrote	Mope

c. Make a list of fifty words containing the "O" sound.

Pay attention to the way in way in which you say these words. Do not try to say the sound before your lips are in the correct position.

d. Work on the following poem:

On First Looking into Chapman's Homer

Much have I travelled in the realms of gold,
And many goodly states and kingdoms seen;
Round many western islands have I been
Which bards in fealty to Apollo hold.
Oft of one wide expanse had I been told
That deep-browed Homer ruled as his demesne:

Yet did I never breathe its pure serene
Till I heard Chapman speak out loud and bold:
Then felt I like some watcher of the skies
When a new planet swims into his ken;
Or like stout Cortez, when with eagle eyes
He stared at the Pacific—and all his men
Look'd at each other with a wild surmise—
Silent, upon a peak in Darien.

—*John Keats.*

6. "A" [eɪ] as in "day."

eɪ

or

ei

LONG "A"

Symbols: LOWER-CASE E/SMALL CAPITAL I
Phonemic Classification: mid-front tense unrounded
IPA usage: "save"; "train"
American English usage: "April"; "weigh"

Here again we have not one vowel sound but a combination of two vowel sounds said as one. Such vowels are called diphthongs.

The secret of saying them well lies largely in opening the mouth sufficiently in shaping the first element to allow the second element to be shaped as the lower jaw moves from this relaxed position back to a partially closed position.

N.B.—There should never be less than half an inch between the upper and lower teeth.

Open the mouth so that a space the width of the thickness of two fingers is made. Place the tongue tip against the lower teeth and attempt to say "A" as in cake. Notice how, as you say the second element of the sound the lower jaw moves up until the space is not more than the width of one finger and the front of the tongue moves up towards the hard palate.

In practicing this sound take care that the lower jaw never becomes rigid. Notice how the glide between the two elements of this sound is much narrower than it was in the case of [oʊ.]

The reason why this sound is often so badly said is that the lower jaw is so rigid that it cannot make the two movements involved. Practice that Yogi exercise again and remember that your mouth must be sufficiently wide open to allow the tongue to make the finely graded transition movements involved.

a. Now practice the following verse, paying particular attention to the shaping of the frequently occurring "A" sounds in the words:

Paula Crane,
Is at it again,
She's trying to crawl through a window-pane.

I know she'll fail,
She's much too big,
From her beak to her tail
She's the size of a whale,
not quite, perhaps,
but the size of a pig.
She's at it again,
Ridiculous Crane,
Who's heard of a Crane through a window-pane?
—D.L.

b. Intone the following words and then say them, giving particular attention to the length of the vowel sound:

Cake	Train	Pale	Table	Stray
Lake	Rain	Fail	Stable	Clay
Make	Plain	Tail	Sable	Gay
Take	Stain	Whale	Cradle	Day
Bake	Grain	Sail	Ladle	May

c. Make a list of fifty words containing the "A" sound.
Pay attention to the way in which you say these words. Do not try to say the sound before your lips are in the correct position.

d. The following poem has been chosen to give you practice in saying this "A" sound.

Waken, Lords and Ladies Gay

Waken, lords and ladies gay!
On the mountain dawns the day,
All the jolly chase is here,
With hawk, and horse, and hunting spear!

Hounds are in their couples yelling,
Hawks are whistling, horns are knelling,
Merrily, merrily, mingle they,
Waken, lords and ladies gay!

Louder, louder chant the lay;
Waken, lords and ladies gay.
Tell them youth, and mirth, and glee,
Run a course as well as we:

Time stern huntsmen, who can baulk,
Staunch as hound, and fleet as hawk?
Think of this, and rise with day,
Gentle lords and ladies gay.
—*Sir Walter Scott.*

7. "I" [aɪ] as in "sight"

aɪ or ai LONG "I"	**Symbol:** LOWER-CASE A/SMALL CAPITAL I **Phonemic classification:** low-central lax unrounded **IPA usage:** "sight"; "light" **American English usage:** "aisle"; "fight"; "shy"

This is also a diphthong.

Before attempting to shape this sound practice the following exercise until you have become aware of the initial and the final position of the lower jaw in shaping this sound.

Ah—ee	Ah—ee	Ah—ee—ah
Mah—ee	Mah—ee	Mah—ee—Mah
Nah—ee	Nah—ee	Nah—ee—Nah
Lah—ee	Lah—ee	Lah—ee—lah

Notice how the lower jaw moves down and then up.

A similar movement is involved in saying the diphthong "I" as in "light". It is a combination of two front vowels, a and ɪ. These vowel sounds are made by using the front of the tongue.

In shaping the second element of this diphthong the tongue tip is raised towards the hard palate. But not quite so high as in the case of "EE". The sound you want is short [ɪ] as in "it".

a. Say the following verse, paying particular attention to the "I" sound in the words in which it occurs.

One night,
I saw the strangest sight,
a tiny light,
Dancing on the lawn.
"It might be a fairy,"
I thought,
"An emerald, or a diamond white
glowing in the night."

And then,
And then, I felt I ought
To creep across the lawn,
tip-toe silently,
And catch that light,
So that I might
Keep it for the world to see.
It twisted, tried to soar,
I caught it, then, before
It slipped away into the night,
I caught it,
Held it tight.
Then

Opening my hand with care,
I gazed at what was lying there.
No fairy lay within my sight,
No sign of emeralds, diamonds
white—
I caught it,
Held it firm,
In my hand,
A glowing worm!

—D.L.

b. Intone the following words and then say them, paying particular attention to the length of the vowel sounds.

Might	Pile	Nine	Nice
Write	While	Whine	Mice
Tight	Style	Time	Price
White	Mile	Shine	Dice
Kite	Fine	Grime	Slice
Diary	Diet	Dynamic	Divide

c. Make a list of fifty words containing the "I" sound.

d. Pay attention to the way in which you say these words. Do not try to say the sound before your lips are in the correct position.

e. Memorize the following poem, which affords excellent practice in the shaping of the vowel sound "I" (aɪ).

The Tiger

Tiger! tiger! burning bright,
In the forests of the night,
What immortal hand or eye
Could frame thy fearful symmetry?

In what distant deeps or skies
Burnt the fire of thine eyes?
On what wings dare he aspire—

What the hand dare seize the fire?

And what shoulder, and what art
Could twist the sinews of thy heart?
And, when thy heart began to beat,
What dread hand? and what dread feet?

What the hammer? what the chain
In what furnace was thy brain?
What the anvil? what dread grasp
Dare its deadly terrors clasp?

When the stars threw down their spears,
And watered heaven with their tears,
Did he smile his work to see?
Did he who made the Lamb make thee?

Tiger! tiger! burning bright
In the forests of the night,
What immortal hand or eye
Dare frame thy fearful symmetry?
—*W. Blake.*

8. "e" [ɛ] as in "bed".

ɛ

SHORT "E"

Symbol: EPSILON
Phonemic classification: open mid-front unrounded
IPA usage: "bed"; "many"; "sweat"
American English usage: "spread"; "friend"

Most people say this sound fairly well, except when they find it followed by the consonant "l", when it tends to be blunted because in the shaping of the consonant sound the tongue is lax.

It is a question of (1) opening the mouth well and (2) flexibility of the front of the tongue which should be raised about a third of the way towards the hard palate.

a. Now practice the following verse, paying particular attention to the shaping of the frequently occurring "e" sounds in the words:

When, oh when,
It is striking ten,
Then—oh, then
That's the moment when
The fairies dance in the glen:
They dance
In the glen at ten.

Then, oh then,
The Hobble-dee men,
Who live on the fen—
Creep to the glen
to snarl and snatter,
These Hobble-dee men,
At the fairies who dance in the glen.

So when, oh when,
It is striking ten,
and
You hear a creek—
Don't listen, don't peek,
For it, may be them—
THOSE HOBBLE-DEE MEN!
—D.L.

b. Intone the following words and then say them, giving particular attention to the length of the vowel sounds:

Bed	Tell	Twelve	Slept	Sweat
Led	Dell	Delve	Crept	Met
Fed	Swell	Health	Wept	Let
Red	Bell	Weather	Fetch	Bet
Said	Quell	Pelf	Wretch	Pet

c. Make a list of fifty words and practice saying them aloud.
d. Practice the following poems, paying particular attention to the "e" sound.

Lines from the Ancient Mariner

"I fear thee, ancient Mariner!
I fear thy skinny hand!
And thou art long, and lank and brown,
As is the ribbed sea-sand.

"I fear thee and thy glittering eye,
And thy skinny hand, so brown"—
Fear not, fear not, thou wedding guest!
This body dropt not down.

Alone, alone, all, all alone,
Alone on a wide, wide sea!
And never a saint took pity on
My soul in agony.

The many men so beautiful!
And they all dead did lie:
And a thousand thousand slimy things
Lived on; and so did I.

I looked upon the rotting sea,
and drew my eyes away:
I looked upon the rotting deck,
And there the dead men lay.

I looked to heaven, and tried to pray:
But or ever a prayer had gusht,
A wicked whisper came, and made
My heart as dry as dust.

I closed my lids, and kept them closed,
And the balls like pulses beat;
For the sky and the sea, and the sea and the sky
Lay like a load on my weary eye,
And the dead were at my feet.

The cold sweat melted from their limbs,
Nor rot nor reek did they;
The look with which they looked at me
Had never passed away.

An orphan's curse would drag to hell
A spirit from on high;
But oh! more horrible than that
Is a curse in a dead man's eye!
Seven days, seven nights, I saw that curse,
And yet I could not die.

The moving moon went up the sky,
And nowhere did abide;
Softly she was going up
And a star or two beside—

Her beams bemocked the sultry main,
Like April hoar-frost spread;

But where the ship's huge shadow lay,
The charmed water burnt alway
A still and awful red.

Beyond the shadow of the ship,
I watched the water-snakes:
They moved in tracks of shining white,
And when they reared, the elfish light
Fell off in hoary flakes.

Within the shadow of the ship
I watched their rich attire:
Blue, glossy green, and velvet black,
They coiled and swam; and every track
Was a flash of golden fire.

O happy living things! no tongue
Their beauty might declare:
A spring of love gushed from my heart,
And I blessed them unaware:
Sure my kind saint took pity on me,
And I blessed them unaware.

The selfsame moment I could pray:
And from my neck so free
The Albatross fell off, and sank
Like lead into the sea.

—S. Coleridge.

An Old Woman of the Roads

O, to have a little house;
To own the hearth and stool and all,
The heaped up sods upon the fire,
The pile of turf against the wall

To have a clock with weights and chains,
And pendulum swinging up and down;
A dresser filled with shining delf,
Speckled and white and blue and brown.

I could be busy all the day,
Clearing and sweeping hearth and floor;
And fixing on the shelf again
My white, and blue, and speckled store!

I could be quiet there at night
Beside the fire and by myself,
Sure of a bed, and loath to leave
The ticking clock and shining delf!

Och! but I'm weary of mist and dark,
And roads where there's never a house or bush.
And tired I am of bog and road,
And the crying wind and the lonesome hush.

And I'm praying to God on high,
And I'm praying Him night and day
For a little house . . . a house of my own,
Out of the wind and the rain's way.
—*Padraic Colum.*

9. "a" [æ] as in bat.

æ SHORT "A"	**Symbol:** ASH **Phonemic classification:** low-front lax unrounded **IPA usage:** "bat"; "catch"; "absolute" **American English usage:** "that"; "ask"; "dance" (also pronounced [a] or [ɑ]

For "a", as in bat, the front of the tongue is raised slightly.

For "e" as in "bet" it is raised about half way towards the hard palate, and for "i", as in "bit", it is raised about five-sixths of the way.

a. Practice the following rhyme, paying particular attention to the shape of the "a" (æ) sound.

Miss M. Bat

Matilda Bat,
wore a tiny hat,
Of the fashion which was the latest.
Her shoes were new,
and her fan was, too,
While her dress was the very sedatest!

She hung all day from an ancient pole,
not very far from a badger hole,
And supped upon apple,
and fresh fried carp,
And played all the night on a golden harp!

One day hammered on the pole,
(Not very far from the badger hole)
Waggled a card saying "POLE TO LET,
RENT: SIX APPLES IN JELLY SET.
OWNER MOVED TO—BANANA TREE.
ENQUIRE—THE VALLEY—
PLANTATION THREE!"

—D.L.

b. Intone the following words and then say them, giving particular attention to the length of the vowel sound:

Bat	Batch	Apple	Ran
Cat	Thatch	Absolute	Can
Gnat	Latch	Abbey	Van
Sat	Catch	Attic	Ban
And	Sand	Land	Band

c. Make a list of fifty words containing this sound.

d. Memorize the following poem. Do not try to learn the words silently. They are given for practice in speaking aloud. Listen to the sounds all the time and remember to open your mouth on every syllable. If you are not doing this well, then go back to the practice of intoning the poem before you say it. When you say it, remember it means something. See the pictures the words make.

Ozymandias

I met a traveller from an antique land
Who said: "Two vast and trunkless legs of stone
Stand in the desert. Near them on the sand,
Half sunk, a shattered visage lies, whose frown

And wrinkled lip and sneer of cold command
Tell that its sculptor well those passions read
Which yet survive, stamped on these lifeless things,
The hand that mocked them and the heart that fed.

And on the pedestal these words appear:
'My name is Ozymandias, king of kings:
Look on my works, ye mighty, and despair!'
Nothing beside remains. Round the decay
Of that colossal wreck, boundless and bare,
The lone and level sands stretch far away."
—P. B. Shelley.

10. "ɪ" [ɪ] as in "pit".

ɪ SHORT "ɪ"	**Symbol:** SMALL CAPITAL I **Phonemic classification:** high-front lax unrounded **IPA usage:** "pit"; "written"; "milk" **American English usage:** "bit"; "symbol"

A description of the position of the tongue in saying this sound has been given in lesson 8. If this sound is blunt it is because you have a rigid jaw or a flaccid tongue. Go back and do your lip and tongue exercises.

a. Say the following verse, paying particular attention to the "ɪ" sound in the words in which it occurs:

Millicent Finnigan Wilhelmina Trout
(very, very scaly, and,
very, very stout),
Swam in a pond and wished a wish
For a very juicy fly,
on a solid golden dish.

A tiny fairy fish,
heard her wish,
And waved her wand,
and to the pond,
There came a man,
With a bright tin can,
a hook, a line,
And an artificial fly,
Made very cunningly, to catch a fish's eye.

Millicent Finnigan Wilhelmina Trout
(very, very scaly, and,
very, very stout),
Swam in the pond and wished her wish,
When suddenly above her, she heard a—
Swissssssh!
And then close by,
flashed a fly,
What a fly!
Oh my!

There was no golden dish,
To complete this wish,

But with scarcely a look,
She snapped, and the hook,
It was golden, caught her lip,
Caught her lip—flip . . . fliiiiiiip!
She was pulled from the pond,
To the bank beyond.
Just a poor silver trout,
Who wished a wish,
For a fly on a dish!

—*D.L.*

b. Intone the following words and then say them, paying particular attention to the length of the vowel sounds:

Pit	Pink	Kitten	Milk	Pin
Bit	Wink	Mitten	Silk	Bin
Sit	Think	Written	Witch	Sin
Lit	Sink	Bitten	Which	Din

c. Make a list of fifty words containing the "ɪ" sound.

d. Practice saying the following poems aloud until you know them by heart.

Midnight

Midnight's bell goes ting, ting, ting, ting,
Then dogs do howl, and not a bird does sing
But the nightingale, and she cries twit, twit, twit.
Owls then on every bough do sit;
Ravens croak on chimneys' tops;
The cricket in the chamber hops,
And the cats cry mew, mew, mew,
The nibbling mouse is not asleep,
But he goes peep, peep, peep, peep,
And the cats cry mew, mew, mew,
And still the cats cry mew, mew, mew.

—*T. Middleton.*

Overheard on a Salt Marsh

Goblin: Nymph, Nymph, what are your beads?
Nymph: Green glass, Goblin. Why do you stare at them?
Goblin: Give them me.
Nymph: No.
Goblin: Give them me. Give them me.
Nymph: No.
Goblin: Then I will howl all night in the reeds,
Lie in the mud and howl for them.
Nymph: Goblin, why do you love them so?

Goblin: They are better than stars or water,
Better than voices of winds that sing,
Better than any man's fair daughter,
Your green glass beads on a silver ring.
Nymph: Hush, I stole them out of the moon.
Goblin: Give me your beads, I want them.
Nymph: No.
Goblin: I will howl in a deep lagoon
For your green glass beads,
I love them so.
Give them me. Give them.
Nymph: No.

—Harold Munro.

The Little Dancers

Lonely, save for a few faint stars, the sky
Dreams; and lonely, below, the little street
Into its gloom retires, secluded and shy.
Scarcely the dumb roar enters this soft retreat;
And all is dark, save where come flooding rays
From a tavern window: there, to the brisk measure
Of an organ that down in an alley merrily plays,
Two children, all alone and no one by,
Holding their tattered frocks, through an airy maze
Of motion, lightly threaded with nimble feet,
Dance sedately: face to face they gaze,
Their eyes shining, grave with a perfect pleasure.

—Laurence Binyon.

11. "OY" [ɔɪ] as in "boy."

ɔɪ

or

ɔi

"AW-EE"

Symbol: OPEN O/SMALL CAPITAL I

Phonemic classification: mid-back lax rounded, glides to high-front tense rounded

IPA usage: "boy"; "oyster"; "coin"

American English usage: "soil"; "point"; "hoist"

Two movements of the lower jaw and the tongue are involved in this sound. It is a diphthong. The lower jaw is well opened and then contracts slightly. The base of the tongue begins by being raised slightly towards the soft palate, and then as the lower jaw moves up again, the front of the tongue is raised towards the hard palate.

It is a combination of the "AW" sound in "caught" and the short "i" sound in "it." Practice these two pure vowel sounds separately and then "glide" them together.

Aw—i Aw—i Aw—i

a. Say the following verse, paying particular attention to the "OY" sound in the words in which it occurs.

An oyster coughed in a noisy way,
and hoisted himself from his cloister,
he lamented aloud in an oily voice,
"Oh dear, oh dear,
if I had my choice,
I'd never be an oyster.
To live in the sea,
which bubbles and boils,
Upsetting my shell,
and upsetting my toils,
For the moisture's too much for my pretty pink pearl,
it's developed a point, and a sort of a curl,"
Then he sobbed, and his tears fell into the sea,
"Oh won't someone please change places with me?"

—D.L.

b. Intone the following words and then say them, paying particular attention to the length of the vowel sounds.

Boy	Oyster	Noise	Oil	Foist
Toy	Moisture	Coin	Toil	Hoist
Coy	Cloister	Voice	Boil	Joist
Gloy	Roister	Point	Soil	Moist

c. Make a list of fifty words containing the "OY" sound.

d. Pay attention to the way in which you say these words. Do not try to say the sound before your lips are in the correct position.

e. Say the following poems aloud so often that you know them by heart.

Portrait of a Machine

What nudity as beautiful as this
Obedient monster purring at its toil;
These naked iron muscles dripping oil,
And the sure-fingered rods that never miss?

This long and shining flank of metal is
Magic that greasy labour cannot spoil;
While this vast engine that could rend the soil
Conceals its fury with a gentle hiss.
It does not vent its loathing, it does not turn
Upon its makers with destroying hate.
It bears a deeper malice; lives to earn
It's master's bread and laughs to see this great
Lord of the earth, who rules but cannot learn,
Become the slave of what his slaves create.
—Louis Untermeyer.

A Hundred Years Hence

Let us drink and be merry, dance, joke and rejoice,
With claret and sherry, theobo and voice !
The changeable world to our joy is unjust,
All treasure's uncertain,
Then down with your dust!
In frolics dispose your pounds, shillings and pence,
For we shall be nothing a hundred years hence.

We'll sport and be free with Moll, Betty and Dolly,
Have oysters and lobsters to cure melancholy:
Fish-dinners will make a man spring like a flea,
Dame Venus, love's lady,
Was born of the sea;
With her and with Bacchus we'll tickle the sense,
For we shall be past it a hundred years hence.

Your most beautiful bride who with garlands is crown'd
And kills with each glance as she treads on the ground,
Whose lightness and brightness doth shine in such splendour
That none but the stars
Are thought fit to attend her,
Though now she be pleasant and sweet to the sense,
Will be damnably mouldy a hundred years hence.
Then why should we turmoil in cares and in fears,
Turn all our tranquill'ty to sighs and to tears?
Let's eat, drink, and play till the worms do corrupt us,
'Tis certain Post Mortem
Nulla voluptas,
For health, wealth and beauty, wit, learning and sense,
Must all come to nothing a hundred years hence.
—T. Jordan.

12. "U" [ʌ] as in "r<u>u</u>b".

ʌ
"UH"

Symbol: TURNED V
Phonemic classification: mid-back unrounded
IPA usage: "<u>u</u>s"; "m<u>o</u>ther"; "tr<u>ou</u>ble"
American English usage: "bl<u>oo</u>d"; "cr<u>u</u>sh"; "b<u>u</u>bble"

The lower jaw should be well relaxed and the base of the tongue slightly raised and advanced.

The lips are in a neutral position.

a. Say the following verse, paying particular attention to the "U" sound in the words in which it occurs.

The Cow moo'd,
"My butter
Is utterly utter—
It's utterly utterly fine,
When I see it spread
On slices of bread,
I feel really proud it is mine."
The Ram baa'd,
"Your butter
Is possibly utter,
But my mutton is better by points,
Still,
I will not allow,
As proof to a cow,
That a butcher should serve me as joints!"
—*D.L.*

b. Intone the following words and then say them, paying particular attention to the length of the vowel sounds.

Bud	Rub	Rush	Putt	Mutton
Dub	Sud	Crush	But	Button
Cub	Cud	Lush	Cut	Cuddle
Tub	Mud	Plush	Rut	Cousin
Trouble	Bubble	Stubble	Puddle	Double

c. Make a list of fifty words containing the "U" sound.

d. Pay attention to the way in which you say these words. Do not try to say the sound before your lips are in the correct position.

e. "The Thrush's Nest" contains a number of short "U" sounds. Read the poem through and underline the words in which the sound occurs. Then practice the poem aloud.

The Thrush's Nest

Within a thick and spreading hawthorn bush
That overhung a molehill large and round,
I heard from morn to morn a merry thrush
Sing hymns to sunrise, and I drank the sound

With joy; and often, an intruding guest,
I watched her secret toil from day to day—
How true she warped the moss, to form a nest,
And modelled it within with wood and clay;

And by and by, like heath bells gilt with dew,
There lay her shining eggs, as bright as flowers,
Ink-spotted over shells of greeny blue;
And there I witnessed in the sunny hours

A brood of Nature's minstrels chirp and fly,
Glad as the sunshine and the laughing sky.
—John Clare.

13. "ᴜ" [ʊ] as in "pull."

ʊ

or

U

SHORT "OO"

Symbol: UPSILON or SMALL CAPITAL U
Phonemic classification: high-back lax rounded
IPA usage: "pull"; "book"; "cushion"
American English usage: "foot"; "should"; "wolf"

This is also a back vowel. The mouth should be well open and the lips well rounded. The base of the tongue is raised high towards the soft palate and slightly advanced from the back position.

a. Practice the following verses:

Near a bush an Ant was fishing, with a line and hook,
He was munching grains of sugar
and reading from a book.
A bull nearby bellowed,
"PULL
PULL
PULL

Look! you've got a bite,
I know you've got a bite,
Oh don't delay a moment, Ant,
PULL
PULL
PULL."
The Ant looked up from reading—
"What's the fuss, Oh Bull?
Why the bellowing so loudly,
PULL
PULL
PULL?
I'm not fishing now for fish,
On my hook there hangs a dish,
Of the weakest sugared tea,
which I'm keeping cool, you see."

b. Intone the following words and then say them, paying particular attention to the length of the vowel sounds.

Pull	Book	Stood
Wool	Rook	Wood
Could	Took	Butcher
Should	Look	Cushion
Would	Sugar	Bush

c. Make a list of fifty words containing the short "U" sound.

Some people confuse this sound with the previous sound. If this is the case, remember that "U" in "rub" is a much more open vowel sound. The base of the tongue is only slightly raised in shaping the vowel sound in rub, while in shaping the vowel sound "U" as in "pull", the base of the tongue is raised five-sixths of the way towards the soft palate.

Practice saying the following groups of words till you learn to distinguish the two vowel sounds.

Mushroom	Cushion
Rush	Bush
Sugar	Shuffle
Butcher	Mutton
Look	Lucky
Nook	Huckster
Took	Tuck

Say the following verse, paying particular attention to the "U" sound in the words in which it occurs.

Sonnet

O Friend! I know not which way I must look
For comfort, being, as I am, opprest
To think that now our life is only drest
For show; mean handiwork of craftsman, cook,

Or groom. We must run glittering like a brook
In the open sunshine, or we are unblest;
The wealthiest man among us is the best:
No grandeur now in Nature or in book

Delights us. Rapine, avarice, expense,
This is idolatory; and these we adore:
Plain living and high thinking are no more.

The homely beauty of the good old cause
Is gone; our peace, our fearful innocence,
And pure religion breathing household laws.
—W. Wordsworth.

14. "a" [ə] as in "about."

ə

SHORT "UH"

Symbol: SCHWA
Phonemic classification: mid-central lax unrounded
IPA usage: "about"; "the"; "ahead"
American English usage: same as IPA

Usually no difficulty is experienced in shaping this sound. It is made with a well opened mouth, lips in a neutral position, i.e., neither drawn back nor pursed, and the mid-part of the tongue raised about a third of the way towards the middle of the palate.

a. Say the following verse, paying particular attention to the short "uh" sound in the words in which it occurs.

Around, about,
Now in, now out,
Away across the paddock,
The ass chased the donkey
and the donkey chased the haddock.

The antelope was acting as the audience,
while the bird,
watched for a-while—then announced "It's absurd,

The ass chasing the donkey
and the donkey chasing the haddock,
helter skelter, here and there,
around, about the paddock!"

The haddock gasped—
"Alas, alack—
Alas, alack-a-day",
Then falling on his haddock back,
he vanished clean away.

The ass stopped,
the donkey stopped,
while from the tree the bird
said—
"I can't believe it,
it's really quite absurd,
in fact, it's quite fantastic,
for a very healthy haddock . . .
To moan,
"Alas, alas! alack,
and vanish from a paddock!"

—D.L.

b. Intone the following words and then say them, paying particular attention to the length of the vowel sounds.

Around	Agree	The
Aground	Alight	Adieu
Astern	Ahoy	Ahead
About	Alas	

c. Make a list of fifty words containing the short "uh" sound and practice these words, saying them not to yourself but aloud.

d. Pay attention to the way in which you say these words. Do not try to say the sound before your lips are in the correct position.

N.B.—This is the vowel sound heard in "th<u>e</u>" when it occurs before a word with an initial consonant.

Th<u>e</u> dog. Th<u>e</u> horse. Th<u>e</u> man.

The horse and donkey are standing in the meadow.

But when the definite article 'THE' occurs before a word which begins with an initial vowel sound, then the vowel sound in THE is enunciated as long "ee".

Th<u>e</u> apple. Th<u>e</u> arch.

Th<u>e</u> oxen. Th<u>e</u> ass.

Practice the prose passage below, distinguishing carefully the use of the two vowel sounds represented by "THE".

Trees

I like flowering plants, but I like trees more, for the reason, I suppose, that they are slower in coming to maturity, are longer- lived, that you can become better acquainted with them, and that in the course of years, memories and associations hang as thickly on their boughs as do leaves in summer, or fruits in autumn. I do not wonder that great Earls value their trees, and never, save in direst extremity, lift upon them the axe. Ancient descent and glory are made audible in the proud murmur of immemorial woods. There are forests in England whose leafy noises may be shaped into Agincourt, and the names of the battlefields of the Roses; oaks that dropped their acorns in the year that Henry VIII held his field of the Cloth of Gold, and beeches that gave shelter to the deer when Shakespeare was a boy. There they stand, in sun and shower, the broad-armed witnesses of perished centuries; and sore must his need be, who commands a woodland massacre. A great English tree, the rings of a century in its bole, is one of the noblest of natural objects; and it touches the imagination no less than the eye, for it grows out of tradition and a past order of things, and is pathetic with the suggestion of dead generations. Trees waving a colony of rooks in the wind today, are older than historic lines. Trees are your best antiques. There are cedars on Lebanon which the axes of Solomon spared, they say, when he was busy on his temple; there are olives in Olivet that might have rustled in the ears of the Master and the twelve; there are oaks in Sherwood that have tingled to the horn of Robin Hood and have listened to Maid Marian's laugh. Think of the existing Syrian cedar which is nearly as old as history, which was middle-aged before the wolf suckled Romulus; think of the existing English elm in whose branches the heron was reared which the hawks of Saxon Harold killed! If you are a notable, and wish to be remembered, better plant a tree than build a city or strike a medal—it will outlast both!

—From "Dreamsthorp"—Alexander Smith.

15. "o" [ɒ] as in "not."

ɒ

SHORT "O"

Symbol: TURNED SCRIPT A
Phonemic classification: low-back lax half-rounded
IPA usage: "not"; what"
American English usage: "odd"; possible" (also prounounced [a] or [ɑ])

This is a back vowel, that is, to shape it the back of the tongue is raised about one-sixth of the way towards the soft palate. The tongue tip is directly behind the lower teeth. If you do not raise the base of the tongue sufficiently you will get "AH". If you raise it too much you will say "AW". The position of the tongue for producing it is between these two.

a. Say the following verse, paying particular attention to the short "O" sound in the words in which it occurs.

A mummy fox,
A daddy fox,
a tiny little baby fox,

Were playing, very happily,
upon a pile of rocks.

And then a sheep,
Another sheep,
And very soon a flock of sheep,
All gathered round the baby fox,
playing there upon the rocks!

Said one—
"Oh! look, that baby fox,
Do you see, he's wearing socks?
How silly, who has heard of foxes,
Running round in pairs of sockses!"

"Stupid sheep,"
snapped Mrs. Fox,
Those aren't sockses, only socks,
Do you call yourself a flockses,
When you should be called a flock!
—D.L.

b. Intone the following words and then say them, paying particular attention to the length of the vowel sounds.

Lot	Cotton	Hobble	Cobble
Cot	Bottom	Topple	Copper
Hot	Obstacle	Bottle	Knot
Pot	What	Wattle	Modern
Bond	Pond	Wand	Fond

c. Make a list of fifty words containing the short "o" sound.
d. The following poem has a great variety of short vowel sounds and will therefore give you plenty of practice in your effort to perfect them.

The Ballad of Semmerwater

Deep asleep, deep asleep,
Deep asleep it lies,
The still lake of Semmerwater
Under the still skies.

And many a fathom, many a fathom,
Many a fathom below,
In a king's tower and a queen's bower
The fishes come and go.

Once there stood by Semmerwater
A mickle tower and tall:
King's tower and Queen's bower
And the wakeman on the wall.

Came a beggar halt and sore;
"I faint for lack of bread."
King's tower and Queen's bower
Cast him forth unfed.

He knocked at the door of the herdman's cot,
The herdman's cot in the dale.
They gave him of their oatcake,
They gave him of their ale.

He has cursed aloud that city proud,
He has cursed it in its pride;
He has cursed it into Semmerwater
Down the brant hillside;
He has cursed it into Semmerwater,
There to bide.

King's tower and Queen's bower,
And a mickle town and tall;
By glimmer of scale and gleam of fin,
Folk have seen them all.
King's tower and Queen's bower,
And weed and reed in the gloom;
And a lost city in Semmerwater;
Deep asleep till Doom.

—*William Watson.*

16. "EE" [i] as in "need."

i

LONG "EE"

Symbol: LOWER-CASE I
Phonemic classification: high-front tense unrounded
IPA usage: "need"; "mean"; "evil"
American English usage: "bleak"; "machine"; "he"

This is an easy sound to make. It is a front vowel and the front of the tongue is raised as far as it can go towards the hard palate, without making a contact.

a. Say the following verse, paying particular attention to the long "EE" sound in the words in which it occurs:

Have you seen Josephine?
A frog who's tiny, plump and green,
And in between each hop,
she dreams,
A dream of what she might have been.

A peacock—a Fairy Queen.
A radish, or a pint of cream
If you've seen
this frog who's green,
Stop her dreaming in between
each hop,
And send her to our stream.
For though there's lots she might have been,
We like her best—as Josephine!

—D.L.

b. Intone the following words and then say them, paying particular attention to the length of the vowel sounds:

Heed	Mean	Gleam	Bleed
Lead	Bean	Beam	Evil
Seed	Beaver	Stream	Easter
Weed	Beast	Seam	Heave

c. Make a list of fifty words containing the long "EE" sound.
d. Pay attention to the way in which you say these words. Do not try to say the sound before your lips are in the correct position.

Music Comes

Music comes
Sweetly from the trembling string
When wizard fingers sweep
Dreamily, half asleep;
When through remembering reeds
Ancient airs and murmurs creep,
Oboe oboe following,
Flute answering clear high flute,
Voices, voices—falling mute,
And the jarring drums.

At night I heard
First a waking bird
Out of the quiet darkness sing . . .
Music comes
Strangely to the brain asleep!
And I heard
Soft, wizard fingers sweep

Music from the trembling string,
And through remembering reeds
Ancient airs and murmurs creep;
Oboe oboe following,
Flute calling clear high flute,
Voices faint, falling mute,
And low jarring drums;
Then all those airs
Sweetly jangled—newly strange,
Rich with change. . . .

Was it wind in the reeds?
Did the wind range
Over the trembling string;
Into flute and oboe pouring
Solemn music; sinking, soaring
Low to high,
Up and down the sky?
Was it wind jarring
Drowsy far-off drums?
Strangely to the brain asleep
Music comes

—*John Freeman.*

17. "IR" [ɜ] as in "bird."

ɜ

or

ɝ

"ER"

Symbol: British: REVERSED EPSILON; American: RIGHT HOOK REVERSED EPSILON

Phonemic classification: mid-central lax unrounded (with R-shading

IPA usage: "bird"; "lurk"; "early"

American English usage: "squirm"; "search"

The lips are firmly rounded and the blade of the tongue raised about half-way towards the middle of the hard palate. Be careful not to narrow the lip aperture too much or you will sound affected.

a. Say the following verse, paying particular attention to the "ER" sound in the words in which it occurs.

A worm twirled on the ground,
He swirled his tail around,
"I'm up before the early bird has stirred,"
said the worm. "In all the world,

I must be the first awake." He curled
with sheer delight,
in the early morning light.

A little girl
saw the worm,
curling on the ground—
"Oh, Daddy, look, I've found,
a worm." She picked it up, most elated.
"I know we'll catch a fish,
if this worm on the hook,
is baited."

The worm lamented,
"What is worst—
being swallowed by the bird who's first,
or lying lonely on a dish,
waiting to be gobbled by a fish?"
—D.L.

b. Intone the following words and then say them, paying particular attention to the length of the vowel sounds.

World	Girl	Work	Bird
Word	Curl	Quirk	Stirred
Worst	Furl	Lurk	Slurred
Worm	Twirl	Birch	Demurred
	Swirl	Early	

c. Make a list of fifty words containing the "IR" sound.

d. Pay attention to the way in which you say these words. Do not try to say the sound before your lips are in the correct position.

Horses on the Camargue

In the grey wastes of dread,
The haunts of shattered gulls where nothing moves
But in a shroud of silence like the dead,
I heard a sudden harmony of hooves,
And, turning, saw afar
A hundred snowy horses unconfined,
The silver runaways of Neptune's car
Racing, spray-curled, like waves before the wind.
Sons of the Mistral, fleet
As him with whose strong gusts they love to flee,
Who shod the flying thunders on their feet
And plumed them with the snortings of the sea.
Theirs is no earthly breed
Who only haunt the verges of the earth
And only on the sea's salt herbage feed—

Surely the great white breakers gave them birth.
For when for years a slave,
A horse of the Camargue, in alien lands,
Should catch some far-off fragrance of the wave
Carried far inland from his native sands,
Many have told the tale
Of how in fury, foaming at the rein,
He hurls his rider; and with lifted tail,
With coal-red eyes and cataracting mane,
Heading his course for home,
Though sixty foreign leagues before him sweep,
Will never rest until he breathes the foam
And hears the native thunder of the deep.
But when the great gusts rise
And lash their anger on these arid coasts,
When the scared gulls career with mournful cries
And whirl across the waste like driven ghosts:
When hail and fire converge,
The only souls to which they strike no pain,
Are the white-crested fillies of the surge,
And the white horses of the windy plain.
Then in their strength and pride
The stallions of the wilderness rejoice.
They feel their Master's trident in their side,
And high and shrill they answer to his voice.
With white tails smoking free,
Long streaming manes and arching necks, they show
Their kinship to their sisters of the sea—
And forward hurl their thunderbolts of snow.
Still out of hardship bred,
Spirits of power and beauty and delight
Have ever on such frugal pastures fed,
And loved to course with tempests, through the night.
—*Roy Campbell*

18. "AIR" [εə] as in "pair."

εə

or

ɛɚ

"AIR"

Symbol: EPSILON/SCHWA (RIGHT-HOOK SCHWA)

Phonemic classification: Begins: Mid-front lax unrounded. Glides to mid-central lax unrounded (with R-shading).

IPA usage: "pair"; "where"

American English usage: "air"; "scare"; "there"

The tendency to misshape this sound is widespread. That is because the lower jaw is too tight and you have not remembered that there are two vowel sounds involved, for it is a diphthong.

It is a combination of the vowel sound you hear in "SET" and the neutral vowel sound you hear in "THE".

Open your mouth well and say (ɛ), then allow the lower jaw to move up slightly and the blade of the tongue to move towards the centre palate for ə.

There are two distinct movements of the lower jaw and two distinct movements of the tongue involved.

Lazy speakers try to do it in one. It is a form of labour-saving that is disastrous.

Set—the	Set—the	Set—the
ɛ—ə	ɛ—ə	ɛ—ə
ɛə	ɛə	ɛə
There	There	There

Practice saying:

Hair, care, where, stare, chair, fair

a. Say the following verse, paying particular attention to the "AIR" sound in the words in which it occurs.

The Bear

On a stair,
I meat a bear,
"Are you going anywhere
Mr. Bear?"

He stared a stare,
"You foolish child, you beware,
Of asking me, a busy bear,
If I'm going anywhere.
Of course I am—
the
next
stair
down."
Then he left me with a frown.

If I should meet another bear
walking up or down a stair,
I won't look,
and I won't care
I'll just pretend he isn't there!
—D.L.

b. Intone the following words and then say them, paying particular attention to the length of the vowel sounds.

Pair	Fair	Various	Wary
Stare	Hair	Hilarious	Dairy
Lair	Wear	Nefarious	Chary
Glare	Care	Gregarious	Hairy
There	Where	Mayor	Chair

c. Make a list of fifty words containing the "AIR" sound.

e. Work on the following poem, paying particular attention to the vowel sound "AIR" wherever it occurs.

The Listeners

"Is there anybody there?" said the Traveller,
Knocking on the moonlit door;
And his horse in the silence champed the grasses
Of the forest's ferny floor;
And a bird flew up out of the turret,
Above the Traveller's head:
And he smote upon the door again a second time;
"Is there anybody there?" he said.
But no one descended to the Traveller;
No head from the leaf-fringed sill
Leaned over and looked into his grey eyes,
Where he stood perplexed and still.
But only a host of phantom listeners
That dwelt in the lone house then
Stood listening in the quiet of the moonlight
To that voice from the world of men,
Stood thronging the faint moonbeams on the dark stair,
That goes down to the empty hall,
Hearkening in an air stirred and shaken
By the lonely Traveller's call.
And he felt in his heart their strangeness,
Their stillness answering his cry,
While his horse moved, cropping the dark turf
'Neath the starred and leafy sky;
For he suddenly smote on the door, even
Louder, and lifted his head.
"Tell them I came, and no one answered,
That I kept my word," he said.
Never the least stir made the listeners,
Though every word he spake
Fell echoing through the shadowiness of the still house
From that one man left awake.
Ay, they heard his foot upon the stirrup,

And the sound of iron on stone,
And how the silence surged softly backward,
When the plunging hoofs were gone.
—*Walter de la Mare.*

19. "EAR" [ɪə] as in "fear". You may also see [ir] as in "sincere".

ɪə

or

ɪɚ

or

ir

"EAR"

Symbol: SMALL CAPITAL I/SCHWA

Phonemic classification: Begins: high-front lax unrounded. Glides to: mid-central unrounded.

IPA usage: "fear"; "weir"; "queer"

American English usage: "peer"; "ear"; "sincere"

This is a combination of the short "i" sound heard in "sit" and the neutral vowel sound heard in "the". Remember this is a diphthong and do not forget to say the second part of it. The shaping of the second element involves the retraction of the lower jaw from the lowered position to a slightly more raised position.

a. Say the following verse, paying particular attention to the "EAR" sound in the words in which it occurs.

Emelena Meer-cat,
picked up a cricket bat;
"Let me catch you"
she said to the deer.
she said to the deer.
"Oh dear, Oh dear,
she's getting quite near—
With that bat,
Oh my hat—
Oh dear," said the deer.

But Emelena Meer-cat,
running with that cricket bat:
Tumbled and fell
on her ear—
and I fear,
That the deer turned round—
"How queer,"
said the deer—

"There's Emelena Meer-cat—
Lying very flat, so flat—
Like a red-Indian with her ear to the ground".
—D.L.

b. Intone the following words and then say them, paying particular attention to the length of the vowel sound.

Beer	Hear	Weir	Clear
Steer	Peer	Ear	Mere
Deer	Year	Jeer	Queer
Seer	Near	Austere	Cheer

c. Make a list of fifty words containing the "EAR" sound.
d. Pay attention to the way in which you say these words. Do not try to say the sound before your lips are in the correct position and your mouth well opened.
e. Further practice in the use of this sound will be given by saying the following poems aloud.

The Rain

I hear leaves drinking Rain:
I hear rich leaves on top
Giving the poor beneath
Drop after drop;
'Tis a sweet noise to hear
The green leaves drinking near.

And when the sun comes out,
After this rain shall stop,
A wondrous Light will fill
Each dark, round drop:
I hope the sun shines bright:
'Twill be a lovely sight.
—W. H. Davies.

The River's Song

Clear and cool, clear and cool,
By laughing shallow and dreaming pool,
Cool and clear, cool and clear,
By shining shingle, and foaming weir;
Under the crag where the ouzel sings,
And the ivied wall where the Church bell rings,
Undefiled, for the undefiled,
Play by me, bathe in me, Mother and child.

Dank and foul, dank and foul,
By the smoky town in its murky cowl,

Foul and dank, foul and dank,
By wharf and sewer and slimy bank;
Darker and darker the farther I go;
Baser and baser the richer I grow,
Who dare sport with the sin-defiled?
Shrink from me, turn from me, Mother and child.

Strong and free, strong and free,
The floodgates are open, away to the sea.
Free and strong, free and strong,
Cleansing my streams as I hurry along,
To the golden sand, and the leaping bar,
And the taintless tide that awaits me afar;
As I lose myself in the infinite main,
Like a soul that has sinned and is pardoned again,
Undefiled for the Undefiled;
Play by me, bathe in me, Mother and child.

—Charles Kingsley.

It would be a good plan to begin to make a collection of poems for yourself, grouped under vowel sounds, and to use these to give you practice.

20. "OAR" [ɔə] as in "more".

ɔə

or

ɔɚ

or

ɔr

"OAR"

Symbol: OPEN O/SCHWA (with right-hook schwa)
Phonemic classification: Begins: mid-back lax rounded
Glides to: mid-central rounded
IPA usage: "more"; "shore"; "four"; "story"
American English usage: "ore"; pour, or, door

This is a combination of the "AW" sound heard in "caught" and the neutral sound heard in "the".

a. Say the following verses, paying particular attention to the "OAR" sound in the words in which it occurs.

Four glow-worms saw,
the open door,
of a tiny country store.
"An open door,
oh; let's explore,"
said little glow-worm number four.

They flew right through,
the open door,
Glow-worms, one, two, three and four,
But the door, slammed shut, before,
they had a moment to explore.

And a voice said
"Ah, what more
light do I need," and before
an eye-lid flickered, quick as whist,
the glow-worms lay in a hot fist.

The latest news of these worms four,
who ventured through an open door,
is very sad, I greatly fear,
for they are now a chandelier.

N.B.—Notice that the vowel sound in "s<u>aw</u>" is not the same as the vowel sound in "d<u>oor</u>".

b. Intone the following words and then say them, paying particular attention to the length of the vowel sounds.

More	Door	Lore	Hoary
Bore	Shore	For	Story
Core	Pore	Four	Glory
Store	Tore	Gore	Tory

c. Make a list of fifty words containing the "OAR" sound.
d. Pay attention to the way in which you say these words. Do not try to say the sound before your lips are in the correct position.
e. Note the "OAR" sound where it occurs in the following poem and practice saying the poem till you know it by heart.

In No Strange Land

O world invisible, we view thee,
O world intangible, we touch thee,
O world unknowable, we know thee,
Inapprehensible, we clutch thee!

Does the fish soar to find the ocean,
The eagle plunge to find the air—
That we ask of the stars in motion
If they have rumour of thee there?

Not where the wheeling systems darken,
And our benumbed conceiving soars!—
The drift of pinions, would we hearken,
Beats at our own clay-shuttered doors.

The angels keep their ancient places;—
Turn but a stone and start a wing!
'Tis ye, 'tis your estrangéd faces,
That miss the many-splendoured thing.

But (when so sad thou canst not sadder)
Cry;—and upon thy so sore loss
Shall shine the traffic of Jacob's ladder
Pitched betwixt Heaven and Charing Cross.

Yea, in the night, my Soul, my daughter,
Cry;—clinging Heaven by the hems;
And lo, Christ walking on the water
Not of Gennesareth, but Thames!
—*Francis Thompson.*

21. "OOR" [ʊə] as in "poor." You may also see [ur] as in "tour".

ʊə

or

ʊɚ

or

ur

"OOR"

Symbol: UPSILON/SCHWA (with right-hook schwa).

Phonemic classification: Begins: high-back lax rounded to mid-central lax unrounded.

IPA usage: "poor"; "moor"; "jury"

American English usage: "secure"; "tour"; "poor"

This is a combination of the vowel soŭnd heard in "PULL" and the neutral vowel sound heard in "THE."

Do not make the mistake of saying this as a pure vowel sound. It is a diphthong. Do not be too lazy to say the second part of it. Or, worse still, do not be so unaware of the distinction between sounds as to confuse it with the "aw" sound as in "caught".

a. Say the following words, paying particular attention to the "OOR" sound.

Poor	Moor
Dour	Tour
Boor	Jury

b. Make a list of fifty words containing the "OOR" sound.
c. Pay attention to the way in which you say these words. Do not try to say the sound before your lips are in the correct position.
d. Underline the "OOR" sounds in the following poem before you practice speaking it.

Rosabelle

O listen, listen, ladies gay!
No haughty feat of arms I tell:
Soft is the note, and sad the lay
That mourns the lovely Rosabelle.

"Moor, moor the barge, ye gallant crew!
And, gentle lady, deign to stay!
Rest thee in Castle Ravensheuch,
Nor tempt the stormy Firth today.

"The blackening wave is edged with white;
To inch and rock the sea-mews fly;
The fishers have heard the Water-Sprite,
Whose screams forebode that wreck is nigh.

"Last night the gifted Seer did view
A wet shroud swathed round lady gay;
Then stay thee, Fair, in Ravensheuch;
Why cross the gloomy Firth to-day?

" 'Tis not because Lord Lindesay's heir
To-night at Roslin leads the ball,
But that my lady-mother there
Sits lonely in her castle-hall.

" 'Tis not because the ring they ride,
And Lindesay at the ring rides well,
But that my sire the wine will chide
If 'tis not filled by Rosabelle."

—O'er Roslin all that dreary night
A wondrous blaze was seen to gleam;
'Twas broader than the watch-fire's light,
And redder than the bright moonbeam.

It glared on Roslin's castled rock,
It ruddied all the copse-wood glen;
'Twas seen from Dryden's groves of oak,
And seen from cavern'd Hawthornden.

Seem'd all on fire that chapel proud
Where Roslin's chief uncoffin'd lie,
Each Baron, for a sable shroud,
Sheath'd in his iron panoply.

Seem'd all on fire within, around,
Deep sacristy and altar's pale;
Shone every pillar foliage-bound,
And glimmer'd all the dead men's mail.

Blazed battlement and pinnet high,
Blazed every rose-carved buttress fair—
So still they blaze, when fate is nigh
The lordly line of high Saint Clair.

There are twenty of Roslin's barons bold
Lie buried within that proud chapelle;
Each one that holy vault doth hold,
But the sea holds lovely Rosabelle!

And each Saint Clair was buried there
With candle, with book, and with knell;
But the sea-caves rung, and the wild winds sung
The dirge of lovely Rosabelle.
—Sir Walter Scott.

22. "YEW" as in "few."

ju "YEW"	**Symbol:** LOWER-CASE J/LOWER-CASE U **Phonemic classification:** lingua-palatal glide (semi-vowel) to high back tense unrounded **IPA usage:** "few"; "mule"; "tube" **American English usage:** "union"; "beauty"; "view"

Here we have a combination of the semi-vowel "y" [j] as heard in "yet," and the pure vowel sound OO [u] as in "cool."

To say "y" as in "yet", the edges of the blade of the tongue are against the mid-palate, and there is an elastic recoil from this position as the lower jaw moves down.

Practice saying y—OO—y—oo—y—oo.

Now glide these two sounds together and you will produce the [ju] sound as in "music."

a. Say the following verse and notice that the stress is on the vowel sound "oo", not on the semi-vowel "y":

The Mule played a tune on the lute,
While—
the Pelican blew on a flute.
A note on the bugle was blown,
By a kingfisher, sitting alone—

Upon a puce carpet
spread out on a bough—
While a cricket chirped loudly:
AND
A mournful old cow
Beat with her hooves on a huge rusty tin,
Making a perfectly horrible din—
But they loved every minute of their escapades;
And they learnt, in their way,
how great music is made.

—D.L.

b. Intone the following words, and then say them, paying particular attention to the length of the vowel sounds.

Few	Hugh	Beauty	Suit
Mew	View	Duty	Newt
Stew	Cue	Acute	Astute
Dew	Pew	Obtuse	Neuter
Mule	Tune	Fume	Tube

c. Make a list of fifty words containing the "YEW" [ju] sound.
d. Pay attention to the way in which you say these words. Do not try to say the sound before your lips are in a correct position.
e. Say the following poem aloud, paying particular attention to the "YEW" sound. Say it so often that you know it by heart.

The Kingfisher

It was the Rainbow gave thee birth,
And left thee all her lovely hues;
And, as her mother's name was Tears,
So runs it in thy blood to choose
For haunts the lonely pools, and keep
In company with trees that weep.
Go you, and, with such glorious hues,
Live with proud peacocks in green parks;
On lawns as smooth as shining glass,
Let every feather show its mark;
Get thee on boughs and clap thy wings
Before the windows of proud kings.
Nay, lovely bird, thou art not vain;
Thou hast no proud ambitious mind;
I also love a quiet place
That's green, away from all mankind,
A lonely pool, and let a tree
Sigh with her bosom over me.

—W. H. Davies.

23. "URE" as in "pure."

jʊə

or

jʊɚ

"URE"

Symbol: LOWER-CASE J/UPSILON SCHWA (with right-hook).

Phonemic classification: lingua-palatal glide (semi-vowel) to high-back tense rounded to mid-central lax rounded.

IPA usage: "pure"; "mature"; "fewer"

American English usage: "cure"; "statue"; "furious"

This is the same vowel sound as the one you hear in poor, but it is prefaced by the semi-vowel "y" [j] as in yet. The stress is on the vowel sound, not on the semi-vowel sound.

yoór [jʊə]

a. Say the following verse, paying particular attention to the "URE" sound in the words in which it occurs.

"I can't endure
anyone who's demure,
And to make me feel furious,
Ask questions—
be curious:
LIKE
"Mrs. Cow, are you sure—
That your milk is quite pure:"
OR
"Dear Mrs. Moo,
Tell me, is it quite true—
Your alluring twin horns,
Are nothing but thorns,
Which you tie on securely—
To peep from,
demurely!"

—D.L.

b. Intone the following words and then say them, paying particular attention to the length of the vowel sounds.

Pure	Bureau	Skewer
Cure	Endure	Fewer
Lure	Mature	Furious
Sewer	Stature	Curious

c. Make a list of fifty words containing the "URE" sound.

d. Pay attention to the way in which you say these words. Do not try to say the sound before your lips are in the correct position.
e. Practice this poem aloud, paying particular attention to the words in which the combination of sounds [jʊə] occurs.

Song

Nay but you, who do not love her,
Is she not pure gold, my mistress?
Holds earth aught—speak truth—above her?
Aught like this tress, see, and this tress,
And this last fairest tress of all,
So fair, see, ere I let it fall?
Because, you spend your lives in praising;
To praise, you search the wide world over;
Then why not witness, calmly gazing,
If earth holds aught—speak truth—above her
Above this tress, and this, I touch
But cannot praise, I love so much!
—Robert Browning.

24. "IRE" as in "squire."

aɪə

or

aɪɚ

"IRE"

Symbol: LOWER-CASE A/SMALL CAPTIAL I/SCHWA (with right-hook).

Phonemic classification: Begins: low-central lax unrounded. Glides to: high-front tense unrounded. Ends: mid-central lax unrounded.

IPA usage: "squire"; "retire"; "sire"

American English usage: "fire"; "choir"; "desire

Here we have a combination of the diphthong "AI" (as in nine) with the neutral [ə] (as in about).

a. Practice saying:

i—er	i—er	i—er	ier
fi—er	fi—er	fi—er	fire
wi—er	wi—er	wi—er	wire
ti—er	ti—er	ti—er	tire

b. Make a list of words containing this sound and practice these words aloud:

Fire	Squire	Acquire
Wire	Choir	Retire
Desire	Spire	Sire

c. Practice the following nonsense rhyme and try to make another one yourself:

In Ireland, lived a squire,
who sat before a fire,
and played upon an ancient violin.

A donkey said,
"Please sire,
May I join you on my lyre,
while my brother beats a rhythm on a tin?"
And then, almost before,
the donkey finished, twenty-four
Monkeys organised a monkey choir,
and they sang, as if inspired,
Until they all felt tired,
Then
The donkey got excited—put his hoof right
through the lyer, and the squire—
Poor squire—
clambered up the tallest spire,
to escape the tiring din,
and in peace,
a little peace,
to play his violin!

d. The following poems will give you further practice in saying this sound:

The Sunflowers

Ah sunflower! weary of time,
Who countest the steps of the sun;
Seeking after that sweet golden clime
Where the traveller's journey is done;

Where the Youth pined away with desire,
And the pale Virgin shrouded in snow,
Arise from their graves, and aspire,
Where my Sunflower wishes to go.
—W. Blake.

The Old Ships

I have seen old ships sail like swans asleep
Beyond the village which men still call Tyre
With leaden age o'ercargoed, dipping deep
For Famagusta and the hidden sun
That rings black Cyprus with a lake of fire;

And all those ships were certainly so old
Who knows how oft with sweat and noisy gun,
Questing brown slaves or Syrian oranges,
The pirate Genoese
Hell-raked them till they rolled
Blood, water, fruit and corpses up the hold.
But now through friendly seas they softly run,
Painted the mid-sea blue or shore-sea green,
Still patterned with the vine and grapes in gold.

But I have seen,
Pointing her shapely shadows from the dawn
And image tumbled on a rose-swept bay,
A drowsy ship of some yet older day;
And, wonder's breath indrawn,
Thought I—who knows—but in that same
(Fished up beyond Æea, patched up new
—Stern painted brighter blue—)
That talkative, bald-headed seaman came
(Twelve patient comrades sweating at the oar)
From Troy's doom-crimson shore,
And with great lies about his wooden horse
Set the crew laughing, and forgot his course.

It was so old a ship—who knows, who knows,
And yet so beautiful, I watched in vain
To see the mast burst open with a rose,
And the whole deck put on its leaves again.
—J. E. Flecker.

CHAPTER 6

Voice Production

Human beings invented the spoken word to communicate ideas, so that they could understand themselves more clearly and make other people understand them.

Never forget that when you speak it *must* mean something. Do not make the mistake of cultivating a speech noise, however pleasant, just for its own sake. Speech is not beautiful because it is well produced or because the speaker has spoken with feeling. It is only beautiful when the speaker has such perfect control of his voice production, and his organs of speech, that he can convey completely the idea in his mind, without forcing the listener to become aware of his limitations as a speaker.

We have been working all this time on the physical aspect of speech, but you will remember that speech has intellectual and emotional aspects that also need to be considered.

Read the following poem aloud:

Inversnaid

This darksome burn, horseback brown,
His rollrock highroad roaring down,
In coop and in comb the fleece of his foam
Flutes and low to the lake falls home.

A windpuff-bonnet of fawn-froth,
Turns and twindles over the broth
Of a pool so pitchblack, fell-frowning,
It rounds and rounds Despair to drowning.

Degged with dew, dappled with dew
Are the groins of the braes that the brook treads through,
Wiry heathpacks, flitches of fern,
And the beadbonny ash that sits over the burn.

What would the world be, once bereft
Of wet and wildness? Let them be left,
O let them be left, wildness and wet;
Long live the weeds and the wilderness yet.

— *Gerard Manley Hopkins.*

The subject of this poem is a highland stream of which a striking feature is the color, a rich "horseback brown", dyed from the peat over which it has passed at its source in some highland hillside.

It hurtles over a rocky bed. The swiftness and force of its movement has worn smooth the rocks over which it runs. We know that it is a fairly wide stream because its path is described as a "highroad", and it is no mere trickle of water, for as it moves, it roars, so there must be a great volume of water making a fairly rapid descent. The "rollrock highroad" must be precipitous.

Thus in two lines the poet has told us of the color, the movement, the course, the sound of this "darksome burn". Then as the character of the bed of the stream changes, the tune changes from roaring to "fluting", for now the stream eddies and swirls in little bays and inlets—"in coop and in comb".

Then it flows into a whirlpool. We are not actually told it is a whirlpool. It is "the broth of a pool, so pitchblack, fell-frowning, it rounds and rounds Despair to drowning". The force and terror of its movement is conveyed by association with images of fear. It is "pitchblack," so that its terrors are intensified since they cannot be clearly seen. The word "broth", together with the phrase "pitchblack", conjures up in our minds a picture of a witch's brew in a boiling cauldron, dark and deadly!

"Fell-frowning" reinforces this impression, for the word "fell", derived from the old English "fellan", to kill, associated with frowning, means "threatening death", an idea which is not only associated with witchcraft, but with giants who are "fell-men to their foes", against whose irresistible strength puny man has little hope. This impression is strengthened by the use of the word "despair" in association with the idea of drowning, of being caught in the grip of this terrifying and death-dealing whirlpool.

Our attention is then directed to the surrounding country, wild and natural. The atmosphere is moist, "Degged with dew" and the ferns borne down by the weight of the water. "Dappled" are the stones. We have been following the course of this stream, and now as it moves through the "groins of the braes"—its movement changes. In the opening verse the movement was that of a wild horse plunging and curvetting, now it has slowed down to "a tread", even-paced, slow and steady, for the stream is full and "banked between the braes", a Scottish word for hills. Notice that wonderful image "the groins of the braes". Looking up the valley which affords a vision of hill after hill on either side of the stream, folding in on one another, has reminded the poet of the shape of the human body, where the lower limbs join the trunk. Make a little diagrammatic sketch of the arrangement of these hills, and you will not only see the aptness of the comparison with groins, but the outline of each hill will become clear to you, and you will see where the poet gets the idea of comparing the shape of each bracken-clad hill as it folds in on the other, with a flitch—which you will remember is a side of bacon. He makes us see exactly the shape, and though he does not say so, the color of the hills, for bacon rind is the color of bracken fern in autumn. By using just one word he has given ideas about the form and color of the landscape as well as the season of the year, and conjured up in our minds the homely farming activities of country people, who keep their pigs and cure their own bacon. Do you remember that "windpuff bonnet of fawn froth" on the whirlpool, like the foam on beer? Another homely image conjured up among country ideas lurking in the back of the mind of the reader.

Notice, too, how the impression that it is autumn is reinforced by mentioning "the beadbonny ash that sits over the burn", a sight familiar in the highlands of Scotland where the mountain ash in autumn is remarkable for its brilliant red berries.

Now do you realize how accurate is the poet's use of language? There are some people who say "a poem can mean anything you like". It is true that your interpretation will be as limited as you are, but a poet means exactly what he says. Someone once said, very aptly, that "a poet is a man who uses one word to suppress many". Is not this the case with Gerard Manley Hopkins' use of the word "flitch"?

Look again at the phrase "flitches of fern"—what is a flitch? Why is that a good description of a hillside? Think of the shape. Think of the color. From what position in relation to the stream is the poet seeing the hillside? What shape is a flitch of bacon? What color is a flitch of bacon? What kind of fern is it? What color is the fern? What time of the year is it? Three little words, but how complete a picture they conjure up. How many questions they evoke!

Has the poet tried to give you a detailed picture of the scene, or an impressionistic picture? Name a painter who belongs to the impressionist school. Is it a modern or a medieval way of painting? Is the use of language in this poem new—original—modern?

Do you realize that the poet has put the word "flitch" to a new use in order to evoke in your mind associated ideas of the country, and of country, and of country things, as well as ideas of shape and color?

He has used his imagination and, therefore, to follow him you must exercise your imagination, so that you can learn to perceive, to think and to feel, in order that you may understand.

The poet conveys his enjoyment of this open-air beauty of hill and valley and stream, by reflecting on how poor the world would be if all of this were lost. And he ends with a passionate plea that the weeds and the wilderness should not be destroyed:

> "Let them be left, oh let them be left wildness and wet.
> Long live the weeds and the wilderness yet."

By the use of the words "weeds and wilderness", we are reminded of the trim gardens of civilization, where man decides which plants are weeds and therefore must be destroyed, and of "sorrow barricadoed evermore within the walls of cities", where "under the pavement the live earth aches".

Language is a living thing. Words not only change in meaning but, as new ideas come into the human mind, new words are invented. Think of some new words invented in the last ten years to express new ideas. Poets are often very skilled in using words in a new way, as Gerard Manley Hopkins has done with the word "flitches". He is not only skilled in using words in a new way, but he can make new words: "coin them" is the expression.

Look at the word "twindle". It is a new word. It contains two ideas: "twine" and "dwindle". Thus he has invented one word to express two characteristics of this falling water:

1. That it is twisting.
2. That it is dwindling, or growing less.

Notice how simple is the language of this poem. There are only two words of three syllables. The rest are words of one or two syllables and they come from the Saxon part of our vocabulary. They are well suited to express the world of external nature, as well as the homely aspects of man's experience. They are rough, homespun words coined in the days when words were called into being because their sound re-echoed the sense of the idea they expressed. "Burn, brae, fell-frowning, degged, dappled, coop, comb, groin, brook, beadbonny, weeds, wilderness", they are words that belong to the countryside, and have "the freshness of the early world".

Let us think again of this idea of sound re-echoing sense. Not only does the poet describe the stream but he makes us hear the changes in the sound of the stream. It roars as it hurtles down the rocks. It flutes as it falls to the lake. The idea contained in the word "roaring" is quite different from the idea contained in the word "fluting". The word roar is associated with a strong animal, like a lion. The word fluting is associated with charming and delicate things. Look at the sounds composing these words, for these differences in idea are reinforced by the difference in the speech sounds of the words.

"R" is a boisterous, noisy sound. "AW" is a long vowel, capable of great resonance. "NG" is also a full-toned, resonant sound. At least it is if you have enough breath to hold it and finish it off!

Now notice the sounds in the word "flutes". The consonant sounds are breath consonants, delicate and light. Say these words: "roaring, flutes". It is not an accident that they sound like their meaning. The sound they make helps to convey the ideas the words suggest.

How important it is to speak poetry aloud, this poet knew, for he once told a friend, who said he could not understand his poems, to take a deep breath and say them aloud.

You will notice in the first verse how the demands made on you to use energetically, your whole speech apparatus, are parallelled by the energetic movement of the stream. Notice the energy that is involved in the use of so many voiced plosives—"*d*arksome *b*urn", "horse*b*ack *b*rown", and rolled consonants in "*r*oll*r*ock high*r*oad *r*oa*r*ing down". It is a breathless speed that the stream has. That breathlessness is conveyed by the use of voiced plosives and rolled consonants.

Then notice the change to the liquid "L" and the soft breath consonants "f" and "s" and the musical effect of the change:

The *fl*eece of his *f*oam *fl*utes.
*L*ow to the *l*ake fa*lls* home.

These things are not accidental; they are the deliberate expression of a being keenly alive to "the *sound* of sense".

Go through this poem analyzing the use of consonant and vowel values, until you get to the last verse where the semi-vowel suggests the lapping of water, and its moisture:

Wildness and wet; let them be left—
Long live the weeds and the wilderness yet.

You can know nothing about these things if you do not know the value of speech sounds.

In the rest of this book you will be introduced not only to the value of consonant sounds, but to the intellectual and emotional aspects of speech. With each poem that is given to you for practice in consonants there will be a lesson on the intellectual aspect of speech, and the emotional aspect, on which we have not yet dwelt. Remember words always evoke emotional responses. Learn to know and be able to analyze what these are.

The Emotional Aspect of Speech

Say "Inversnaid" in a lethargic way which conveys that actually the whole thing is a bore, and that you dislike the subject. Then say it as though you enjoyed the experience, and feel the richer for having become aware of the characteristics of that particular mountain stream, and the ideas in the poet's mind associated with the stream. Then decide which of the two ways more adequately communicates the truth of what Gerard Manley Hopkins has expressed.

That is what matters. That when you speak you should convey the whole truth. It is not enough to train yourself to express perfectly the physical aspect of the Spoken Word, or even the intellectual aspect. The whole meaning can be altered if the feeling is falsely or inadequately conveyed.

Also, ask yourself this question: Which of the following feelings are expressed in this poem?

Love	Hate	Indifference
Enjoyment	Boredom	Excitement
Admiration	Scorn	Mawkish sentiment

This is not all that there is to say about this poem. Only a few suggestions have been made to help you appreciate and understand what poetry is, and of what value it is to you.

"A thing of beauty is a joy forever—its loveliness increases" as your understanding deepens. If we are to enjoy poetry, as it can be enjoyed, our whole being must be fully engaged physically, intellectually and emotionally. That is how we live and grow.

CHAPTER 7

Consonant Sounds

You will remember that there are two kinds of speech sounds, vowel sounds, on which the carrying power of the voice depends; and consonant sounds, on which the distinctness of the voice depends. Consonant sounds must be firmly and neatly shaped. This depends on the control of the organs of speech employed in the production of consonants, which are sounds in which there is a complete or partial contact of the organs of speech.

The Organs of Speech

1. The lips.
2. The tongue.
3. The teeth.
4. The hard palate (the front part of the roof of your mouth).
5. The soft palate (the back part of the roof of your mouth).
6. The gums.

If you are to shape the consonants neatly and firmly, you must have a good control of a flexible tongue. If you know that your tongue is flabby and the tip blunt, you must practice the tongue exercises given earlier in this book. Success in shaping consonants depends, as in vowel sounds, on the power to relax the lower jaw. If you try to articulate consonants with your teeth tightly clenched there will not be sufficient space in the oral cavity for the tongue to function properly, and all the consonants, which depend on the freedom of movement of the tongue, and these are the great majority, will sound woolly and indistinct.

This book lists twenty seven consonant sounds, each of which is tabulated below along with the appropriate phonetic symbols.

Consonant Phonetic Symbols

1	p	as in "pipe"	p
2	b	as in "box"	b
3	m	as in "mime"	m
4	w	as in "win"	w
5	wh	as in "whine"	ʍ or hw
6	f	as in "five"	f
7	v	as in "vine"	v
8	th	as in "thin"	θ
9	TH	as in "them"	ð
10	t	as in "tap"	t
11	d	as in "daddy"	d
12	n	as in "nose"	n
13	l	as in "clean"	l
14	L	as in "dull"	ɫ
15a	r	as in "ran"	r
15b	r	as in "heart"	ɹ
16	s	as in "soon"	s
17	z	as in "zoo"	z
18	sh	as in "short"	ʃ
19	zh	as in "pleasure"	ʒ
20	ch	as in "church"	tʃ
21	j	as in "judge"	dʒ
22	y	as in "yet"	y
23	k	as in "king"	k
24	g	as in "glory"	g
25	ng	as in "ring"	ŋ
26	h	as in "horse"	h

Consonants Can Be Classified in Two Ways:

a. According to the quality of breath employed in their production as:
   i. breath consonants, or aspirates, e.g., p, f, t, k.
   ii. Voiced consonants, or vocal, e.g., b, v, d, g.
b. According to the organs of speech employed in their production as:
   i. Labial consonants, e.g., p, b, m, w—[ʍ.]
   ii. Labio-dental consonants, f, v.

iii. Pre-dental consonants, th—[θ.]
th—[ð]
iv. Post-dental consonants, t, d, n, l, ɫ, r, s, z.
v. Palato-alveolar consonants, sh [ʃ], zh [ʒ], ch [tʃ], j [dʒ].
vi. Palatal consonant, j.
vii. Velar consonants, k, g, ng [ŋ].
viii. Glottal consonant, H [h].

How Consonants Are Formed

1. "p" as in "pipe".

p

"p"

Symbol: LOWER-CASE P
Phonemic classification: bilabial voiceless stop-plosive
IPA usage: "pipe"; "copper"
American English usage: same as IPA.

In the shaping of this consonant the lips are, at first, pressed firmly together. The sound follows the separation of the lips, i.e., the breaking of the contact. The sound which follows is a *breath* sound.

a. Exercises to increase the flexibility of the lips.

p p p   p p p   p p p   p
pop pop pop   pop pop pop   pop pop pop   pop
pip pip pip   pip pip pip   pip pip pip   pip
pep pep pep   pep pep pep   pep pep pep   pep
pup pup pup   pup pup pup   pup pup pup   pup
pap pap pap   pap pap pap   pap pap pap   pap
pawp pawp pawp   pawp pawp pawp   pawp pawp pawp   pawp
poop poop poop   poop poop poop   poop poop poop   poop
peep peep peep   peep peep peep   peep peep peep   peep
pipe pipe pipe   pipe pipe pipe   pipe pipe pipe   pipe
pope pope pope   pope pope pope   pope pope pope   pope
pip-pety   pip-pety   pip-pety   pip
pop-pety   pop-pety   pop-pety   pop
pup-pety   pup-pety   pup-pety   pup

b. Make a list of words beginning with this sound, e.g., poop, post, paper.
Make a list of fifty words containing the sound, e.g., upper, supper, topple.
c. Use some of these words in nonsense rhymes similar to the following well-known one about Peter Piper:

Peter Piper picked a peck of pickled peppercorns.
If Peter Piper picked a peck of pickled peppercorns,
Where is the peck of pickled peppercorns Peter Piper picked?

You can make up these rhymes for yourself. Here is a good example of what can be done if you try:

Patricia Partridge,
In a little pink pinafore,
Picking purple pansies,
peeped through a fence and saw,
Pauline Parsley,
waving at a porcupine,
"Hulloa, Mr. Porcupine,
could you please compose a rhyme
About a precocious Pig called Percy,
But don't end the next line with the word Mercy!"

Peter P. Porcupine,
Peered hard for quite a time,
"Parsley," he muttered,
"Parsley green,
Quite the plumpest piece of parsley,
I have ever seen."

So he plucked the parsley quickly,
Smacked his lips,
"Tis good," said he,
"I always think a piece of parsley,
With digestion does agree."

Patricia Partridge,
Panted "Ooooooo"
So great was her horror, that away she flew,
Dropping her pinafore on the ground,
Scattering the pansies all around;

—D.L.

d. The following poem should be studied in connection with the lesson. You should practice it so often that you know it by heart.

There are more ways than one of learning by heart. The best way is first to understand the ideas expressed and get a picture in your mind of the sequence of ideas in the poem.

Pan

Round and about the sordid street,
With grimy face and dusty feet,
Tattered jacket, ragged vest,
And flaunting paper plume for crest,

Laughing lips and shining eyes
—Forget-me-nots from paradise—
And upturned nose impertinent,
With all his tawdry world content—
Pan, of his woodland haunts beguiled,
Is come again, a gutter child,
That lightly trips on twinkling toes,
And through a comb and paper blows
Fantastic music as he goes.
—E. Hamilton Moore.

The following poem will give you further practice in shaping the "p" sound.

At the same time use it to improve your power of visualizing the pictures the words make. Say the poem slowly enough to give you time to see these pictures. Remember no one will be able to see these pictures as you speak, unless you are seeing them in your own mind as you say the words.

A Passer-by

Whither, O splendid ship, thy white sails crowding,
Leaning across the bosom of the urgent West,
That fearest nor sea rising, nor sky clouding,
Whither away, fair rover, and what thy quest
Ah! soon, when Winter has all our vales opprest,
When skies are cold and misty, and hail is hurling,
Wilt thou glide on the blue Pacific, or rest
In a summer haven asleep, thy white sails furling?

I there before thee, in the country that well thou knowest,
Already arrived am inhaling the odorous air:
I watch thee enter unerringly where thou goest,
And anchor queen of the strange shipping there,
Thy sails for awnings spread, thy masts bare;
Nor is aught from the foaming reef to the snow-capp'd grandest
Peak, that is over the feathery palms more fair
Than thou, so upright, so stately, and still thou standest.

And yet, O splendid ship, unhailed and nameless,
I know not if, aiming a fancy, I rightly divine
That thou hast a purpose joyful, a courage blameless,
Thy port assured in a happier land than mine.
But for all I have given thee, beauty enough is thine,
As thou, aslant with trim tackle and shrouding,
From the proud nostril curve of a prow's line
In the offing scatterest foam, thy white sails crowding.
— Robert Bridges.

2. "b" as in "box."

b

"b"

Symbol: LOWER-CASE B
Phonemic classification: bilabial voiced stop-plosive
IPA usage: "box"; "dabble"; "beetle"
American English usage: same as IPA.

This sound reshaped by the lips, in exactly the same way as [p] is shaped. Place your lips together firmly, but not rigidly, and then separate them. The sound of [b] is not the same as the sound of [p]. [b] is what is called a voiced consonant.

Put your fingers lightly on your throat and feel the vibration as you say [b].

[p] is called a breath consonant. Notice the comparative absence of vibration as you say this sound.

a. Exercises to increase the flexibility of the lips:

b b b   b b b   b b b   b
bob bob bob   bob bob bob   bob bob bob   bob
bib bib bib   bib bib bib   bib bib bib   bib
beb beb beb   beb beb beb   beb beb beb   beb
bub bub bub   bub bub bub   bub bub bub   bub
bab bab bab   bab bab bab   bab bab bab   bab
bawb bawb bawb   bawb bawb bawb   bawb bawb bawb   bawb
boob boob boob   boob boob boob   boob boob boob   boob
beeb beeb beeb   beeb beeb beeb   beeb beeb beeb   beeb
bibe bibe bibe   bibe bibe bibe   bibe bibe bibe   bibe
bobe bobe bobe   bobe bobe bobe   bobe bobe bobe   bobe

bib-bety   bib-bety   bib-bety   bib
bob-bety   bob-bety   bob-bety   bob
bub-bety   bub-bety   bub-bety   bub

b. Make a list of words beginning with this sound, e.g., baker, basket, bowl, and repeat these words aloud.

c. Say the following rhyme for practice in shaping this sound.

In a big black gloomy dungeon,
Built below an ancient town,
There once lived a baby beetle,
Who was not born black—but brown!

All his brother Beetles gossiped,
"Brown all over—head to foot—
We will have to brush him blacker,
With the very blackest soot!"

Baby Beetle heard their gossip,
Scuttled hard across the floor,
Scampered fast as he was able—
Up the stairs and through the door!

"Dusting me with blackest soot,
Being black from head to foot—
Why should I pretend to be,
Black, when brown is really me?"

Now he's living in a basket,
Hanging in a basement store
And he's such a happy beetle—
With a wife, and babies four!

d. The poem below will afford you further practice in shaping the sound "b". At the same time, use it to improve your power of visualization. See the pictures that the words make. Never say you cannot understand a poem until you have read it at least three times aloud, putting the right words into each breath group, for otherwise you are destroying the meaning and the shape of the poem.

When we speak we have frequently to replenish our breath, and to do this there must be a pause in our speaking. Be careful not to make these pauses in such a way as to ruin the meaning of the sentence.

The Caged Skylark

As a dare-gale skylark scanted in a dull cage
Man's mounting spirit in his bone-house, mean house, dwells—
That bird beyond the remembering his free fells;
This in drudgery, day-labouring-out life's age.

Though aloft on turf or perch or poor low stage,
Both sing sometimes the sweetest, sweetest spells,
Yet both droop deadly sometimes in their cells
Or wring their barriers in bursts of fear or rage.

Not that the sweet-fowl, song-fowl, needs no rest—
Why, hear him, hear him babble and drop down to his nest,
But his own nest, wild nest, no prison.

Man's spirit will be flesh-bound when found at best,
But uncumbered: meadow-down is not distressed
For a rainbow footing it nor he for his bones risen.
— Gerard Manley Hopkins.

In a sentence, words fall into groups according to their meaning. These groups are called phrases. Pauses must be made between phrases, when the supply of breath can be renewed. Think of the phrasing when you say the following poem:

Amaranth

Beauty forgotten yet is beauty still,
For nothing lovely ever upon earth,
Not Helen's face, nor Alexander's will,
Passing to death, but comes again to birth.

In some new brain the sleeping dust will waken;
Courage and love that conquered and were done,
Called from a night by thought of man forsaken,
Will know again the gladness of the sun.

And all things we have known for beauty here,
All little things fugitive and forgot,
Quick blossoms that have fallen year by year,
Kisses that even the dawn remembered not,
All these are now the judgment that we bring
To know the heart of every lovely thing.
—*John Drinkwater.*

Phrasing is sometimes called punctuation for the ear. You must practice reading aloud until you acquire skill in phrasing, and to do this you must train your eye to travel ahead of the words you are saying, so that you have a grip of the meaning and can convey it.

Phrasing is one of the most important factors in making clear the meaning of what you say or read. Take a pencil and mark with a stroke the places where you would pause in saying *Amaranth.* Do not make a stroke before you experiment to try the effect on the meaning of making a pause in that particular place. For instance, if you pause between "forgotten" and "yet" in the first line, the meaning is that—in spite of the failure of memory—beauty is immortal, because of the influence it has on us, an influence that contributes something to our power to judge, or to perceive. But if you make the pause after "yet", the meaning is altered, and becomes—though memory may temporarily fail, it will one day recall beauty that the mind once perceived. Obviously it was not the author's intention to convey this, for such an interpretation destroys the significance of what follows. You therefore determine from the context what the meaning is. You must have much practice if you are to become skilled in phrasing the prose or poetry you read or speak, so that the author's meaning is perfectly conveyed.

3. "m" as in "<u>m</u>ime."

m "m"	**Symbol:** LOWER-CASE M **Phonemic classification:** bilabial voiced nasal **IPA usage:** "<u>m</u>ime"; "<u>m</u>oon"; "sta<u>mm</u>er" **American English usage:** same as IPA.

[m] is an interesting sound. It is called a liquid consonant, which means that it can be prolonged, and that it has great vocality and resonance.

Place the lips lightly, but firmly, together. Keep the teeth apart.

Now hum. Hummmmmmmm. Hummmmmmmm.

Notice how the sound flows out through the nose. You should be able to feel the vibrations on the top of your head,

Hummmmmm. . . . . Hummmmmm. . . . . hummmmmm.

Replenish your breath ten times, and remember to use the abdominal press so that you produce a steadily vibrating column of sound.

a. Exercises to increase the resonance of this sound:

m m m	m m m	m m m
mom mom mom	mom mom mom	mom mom mom
mim mim mim	mim mim mim	mim mim mim
mem mem mem	mem mem mem	mem mem mem
mum mum mum	mum mum mum	mum mum mum
mam mam mam	mam mam mam	mam mam mam
mawm mawm mawm	mawm mawm mawm	mawm mawm mawm
moom moom moom	moom moom moom	moom moom moom
meem meem meem	meem meem meem	meem meem meem
mime mime mime	mime mime mime	mime mime mime
mome mome mome	mome mome mome	mome mome mome
mim-mety	mim-mety	mim-mety mim
mom-mety	mom-mety	mom-mety mom
mum-mety	mum-mety	mum-mety mum

b. Make a list of words beginning with this sound, e.g., murmur, moist, moveless, mountain.

c. Repeat the following nonsense rhyme:

Emanuel Mole,
and his Mother Miranda,
Meandered together
along the verandah:
"Emanuel dear—
I'm glad that you are"

(murmured Miranda,
a loving Mama).
"I'm glad that you are a typical Mole,
Not a miserable mouse,
or a stumbly foal:
Not a mumbley bee—
a mink
or a freesia,
Not a mushroom
a mango
a milk-of-magnesia!
I'm really so pleased
that you are what you are,"
Murmured Miranda,
the loving Mama.

—D.L.

d. The following verses not only give you good practice in the shaping of "m" sounds, but are excellent for improving resonance. Try not to shout, use your natural pitch, and increase the power and vitality of your voice by concentrating on the correct method of breathing.

Keep your shoulders down, your chest up, and use the abdominal press while you are speaking:

Sam

When Sam goes back in memory,
It is to where the sea
Breaks on the shingle, emerald-green
In white foam, endlessly;
He says—with small brown eye on mine—
'I used to keep awake,
And lean from my window in the moon,
Watching those billows break
And half a million tiny hands,
And eyes, like sparks of frost,
Would dance and come tumbling into the moon,
On every breaker tossed.
And all across from star to star,
I've seen the watery sea,
With not a single ship in sight,
Just ocean there, and me;
And heard my father snore . . . and once
As sure as I'm alive,
Out of those wallowing, moon-flecked waves
I saw a mermaid dive;

Head and shoulders above the wave;
Plain as I now see you,
Combing her hair, now back, now front,
Her two eyes peeping through;
Calling me, "Sam!"—quietlike—"Sam!" . . .
But me. . . . I never went,
Making believe I kind of thought
'Twas someone else she meant. . . .
Wonderful lovely there she sat,
Singing the night away,
All in the solitudinous sea
Of that there lonely bay.
P'raps,' and he'd smooth his hairless mouth,
'P'raps, if 'twere now, my son,
P'raps, if I heard a voice say, "Sam!" . . .
Morning would find me gone!'
—*Walter de la Mare.*

Remember, of course, about breath control and phrasing, but attention to these alone will not ensure your success in interpreting prose or poetry. You *must* now think of inflection.

Inflection is the rising and falling of the voice. At the end of a sentence, when the meaning is complete, you naturally use a falling inflection, but to use a falling inflection on the last word of every phrase not only makes what you say sound appallingly monotonous, but it makes it impossible to convey the meaning.

In this poem "Sam", which you have been practicing for the improvement of your "m" sound, and for skill in phrasing, notice how often the meaning is not completed at the end of a line but runs on to the next line. This is the case with the second line and the third.

It is to where the sea
Breaks on the shingle, emerald green,
In white foam, endlessly.

The meaning is not complete until the word "endlessly" and yet to maintain the rhythm there must be a pause at "sea" and "green". The secret of saying this well is to observe the pause, but avoid the use of a falling inflection. It requires good breath control.

In every line, more properly called verse, of poetry, there is a rhythmic pause at the end of the line (verse), and it is necessary to observe this pause to keep the pattern of the rhythm. This pause is known as the suspensory pause.

The majority of people when they are reading or speaking poetry are very monotonous and dull to listen to. One of the reasons for this is because they always use a falling inflection with the suspensory pause, whether or not the meaning of the words justifies the falling inflection. It is not a very intelligent thing to do, so do not make this mistake.

Now is the time to develop your technical skill and your imagination, and this is one of the ways, so practice hard, until you are expert in handling the suspensory pause when the meaning overflows the verse.

N.B.—There are many words for this feature of poetry. Sometimes such a verse of poetry is called an enjambed, or run-on, verse.

Remember that the term "verse" is being used in its correct sense as a line, not a stanza, of poetry.

4. "w" as in "win."

w

"w"

Symbol: LOWER-CASE W
Phonemic classification: bilabial slide (semi-vowel)
IPA usage: "win"; "one"; "quickly"
American English usage: same as IPA.

For this sound the lips are rounded as for the vowel sound "oo", and the ["w"] sound is produced by the elastic recoil of the lips from this position.

a. Exercises to increase the flexibility and precision of the lip movements:

w w w	w w w	w w w	w
wow wow wow	wow wow wow	wow wow wow	wow
wi wi wi	wi wi wi	wi wi wi	wi
we we we	we we we	we we we	we
waw waw waw	waw waw waw	waw waw waw	waw
woo woo woo	woo woo woo	woo woo woo	woo
woppety	woppety	woppety	wop
wippety	wippety	wippety	wip
weppety	weppety	weppety	wep

b. Make a list of words beginning with this sound and practice saying these words aloud, e.g., weird, Wednesday, water.

c. Repeat the following nonsense verses:

The Whale, Wallaby and Walrus

In Wales, lived a whale,
and a tiny wallaby:
Who wallowed all the day,
Beneath an ancient walnut tree.
Mr. William Walter Walrus, also used to stay,
In a tiny little wig-wam,
not very far away.
While high upon a windmill,
Lived a winsome little wren,

Who warbled very prettily,
each day from eight to ten.
AND
The whale,
and his friend the little wallaby
stopped wallowing, beneath the ancient walnut tree:
While the Walrus left his wig-wam,
Joined the other two, and then,
Stood beneath the windmill,
and listened to the wren—
Were quite enraptured every day,
from eight o'clock to ten!

—D.L.

The Song of the Wondering Aengus is not an easy poem to say. If you are to do it well you will have to pay attention not only to breath control but to the phrasing and to the inflections you use. This poem is a test of your understanding and imagination. Say it aloud, often.

The Song of Wandering Aengus

I went out to the hazel wood,
Because a fire was in my head,
And cut and peeled a hazel wand,
And hooked a berry to a thread:

And when white moths were on the wing,
And moth-like stars were flickering out,
I dropped the berry in a stream
And caught a little silver trout.

When I had laid it on the floor
I went to blow the fire a-flame,
But something rustled on the floor,
And some one called me by my name;

It had become a glimmering girl
With apple blossom in her hair
Who called me by my name and ran
And faded through the brightening air.

Though I am old with wandering
Through hollow lands and hilly lands,
I will find out where she has gone,
And kiss her lips and take her hands;

And walk among long dappled grass,
And pluck till time and times are done
The silver apples of the moon,
The golden apples of the sun.

i. Tell in your own words the story.
ii. Is this an ordinary or an extraordinary adventure to have?
iii. Do you think there is another meaning in this poem apart from the story of the adventure?

Remember this poem until later, when we shall come back to this question of the obvious meaning, which we shall call the *direct* meaning, and the symbolic meaning, which is sometimes called the "oblique" meaning.

The following poem will afford you good practice for the "w" sound. It is very important to learn to finish off final consonants. You will never speak distinctly until you do! Think about this as you say the following poem:

Extract from the Forsaken Merman

Come, dear children, let us away;
Down and away below!
Now my brothers call from the bay,
Now the great winds shoreward blow;
Now the salt tides seaward flow;
Now the wild white horses play,
Champ and chafe and toss in the spray,
Children dear, let us away!
This way, this way!
Call her once before you go—
Call once yet
In a voice that she will know;
"Margaret! Margaret!"
Children's voices should be dear
(Call once more) to a mother's ear:
Children's voices, wild with pain—
Surely she will come again!
Call her once and come away;
This way, this way,
"Mother dear, we cannot stay!
The wild horses foam and fret."
Margaret! Margaret!
Come away, away, children;
Come, children, come down!
The hoarse wind blows colder;
Lights shine in the town.
She will start from her slumber
When gusts shake the door;

She will hear the winds howling,
Will hear the waves roar.
We shall see, while above us
The waves roar and whirl,
A ceiling of amber,
A pavement of pearl.
Singing: "Here comes a mortal,
But faithless was she!
And alone dwell for ever
The kings of the sea."
—*Matthew Arnold.*

5. "wh" as in "whine."

ʍ

or

hw

SOFT "WH"

Symbol: TURNED W (not used in USA)
Phonemic classification: bilabial voiceless glide
IPA usage: "whine"; "whey"; "which"
American English usage: "whenever"; "whistle"; "wheel"

This sound is said in the same way as [w], but it is preceded by a forcible expulsion of breath, in fact, by the "h" sound.

a. Exercises:

wh wh wh　　wh wh wh　　wh wh wh
whop whop whop　　whop whop whop　　whop whop whop
whip whip whip　　whip whip whip　　whip whip whip
whup whup whup　　whup whup whup　　whup whup whup
whap whap whap　　whap whap whap　　whap whap whap
whoop whoop whoop　　whoop whoop whoop　　whoop whoop whoop
weep weep weep　　weep weep weep　　weep weep weep
whip-pety　　whip-pety　whip-pety　　whip
whop-pety　　whop-pety　whop-pety　　whop
whup-pety　　whup-pety　whup-pety　　whup

b. Make a list of words beginning with initial w, and another list beginning with initial ʍ:

Wine	Whine
Witch	Which
Wistful	Whistle
Wet	Whet
Way	Whey
Weal	Wheel

c. Say the following sentence:

"Which witch whistled, and which witch whined, at the loss of the whey on which they dined?"

d. Make up nonsense verses which will test your skill in the shaping of these two sounds.

A whisk
whisked an egg,
with a whisk,
and a whisk,
and a whisk,
Till the egg wasn't yellow,
It was white
quite white—
with fright!
From a hill,
Whip-poor-will,
Flew with a whir—and whistled—
"Oh, owl, Mr. Owl, listen well
for a-while,
A fowl laid that egg!"
"Whooo?" said the Owl,
"A fowl?
Let it whisk
Till it's white—
It's best that it whirls in a cake,
to bake,
Than hatch to a fowl,
Silly fowl,"
Said the Owl.

—D.L.

e. Practice the following poem:

Tewkesbury Road

It is good to be out on the road, and going one knows not where,
Going through meadow and village, one knows not whither or why;

Through the grey light drift of the dust, in the keen cool rush of the air,
Under the flying white clouds, and the broad blue lift of the sky;

And to halt at the chattering brook, in the tall green fern at the brink
Where the harebell grows, and the gorse, and the foxgloves purple and white;

Where the shy-eyed delicate deer troop down to the pools to drink
When the stars are mellow and large at the coming on of the night.

O, to feel the warmth of the rain, and the homely smell of the earth,
Is a tune for the blood to jig to, a joy past power of words;

And the blessed green comely meadows seem all a-ripple with mirth
At the lilt of the shifting feet and the dear wild cry of the birds.

—*John Masefield.*

Say it as though you were telling somebody how you feel about the pleasure of walking in the country. See the pictures and feel the emotions that the poet expresses.

You have five senses

1. The sense of *touch.*
2. The sense of *taste.*
3. The sense of *smell.*
4. The sense of *sight.*
5. The sense of *hearing.*

Which of these senses do you consider the most important?

Which would you least like to do without?

Find proof in this poem that the poet who wrote it is alert in his five senses, by choosing five images that he mentions, each of which appeals to one of the senses.

Poetry should make you more aware of the world about you. When you read poetry ask yourself what are the things of which the poet is aware.

Answer the following questions:

1. What is the loveliest thing you have ever seen?
2. What is the most delicious thing you have ever tasted?
3. What is the most pleasant sound you have ever heard?
4. What appeals to your sense of touch?
5. What is the most fragrant smell you know?

To which of your senses do the following appeal:

1. Light and shadow on trees.
2. The bloom on a plum.
3. Fresh paint.
4. A rainbow.
5. Geranium leaves.
6. Grapes.
7. White sails on the bay.
8. Dripping leaves.
9. Dappled stones.
10. Dew-drenched gossamer.
11. Ice cream.
12. Ivory.
13. Marble.
14. The whistle of a train.
15. A kitten.
16. Pearls.
17. Frangipani.
18. Apples.
19. Wood smoke.
20. Pattering feet.
21. Camphor wood.
22. Crickets chirping.

Is it of any value to be alive in your five senses? Give reasons for your answer.

6. "f" as in "five."

f

"F"

Symbol: LOWER-CASE F
Phonemic classification: Labio-dental voiceless fricative
IPA usage: "five"; "off "; "photograph"; tough"
American English usage: Same as IPA.

This consonant is known as a labio-dental, because the sound follows the release of the contact of the upper teeth with the lower lip.

[f] is a breath, or aspirate consonant.

a. Exercises for "f" as in "*f*ive."

f f f	f f f	f f f	f
fif fif fif	fif fif fif	fif fif fif	fif
fof fof fof	fof fof fof	fof fof fof	fof
fuf fuf fuf	fuf fuf fuf	fuf fuf fuf	fuf
fiv fiv fiv	fiv fiv fiv	fiv fiv fiv	fiv
fov fov fov	fov fov fov	fov fov fov	fov
fuv fuv fuv	fuv fuv fuv	fuv fuv fuv	fuv
fiffety	fiffety	fiffety	fiv
faffety	faffety	faffety	fav
feffety	feffety	feffety	fef

b. Make a list of fifty words beginning with "f", e.g., five, find, fix, fluffy, frantic.
c. Make up nonsense rhymes that will afford exercise in attaining agility in the shaping of this sound and practice aloud.

Florence Fox,
Became quite fascinated,
With a fashion magazine,
(Unfortunately dated),
Showing photographs of feathered cuffs,
Together with fantastic muffs,
To please the most fastidious,
The most fastidious little fox,
Who ever flaunted fluffy socks,
or, snuggled to the nose, in her
Most expensive foxs' fur!

—*D.L.*

d. The poem chosen for practice is a seventeenth century sonnet. Read it through carefully, taking great care to phrase properly, and to use the right inflections. Remember the meaning matters more than anything else.

A Rose

Blown in the morning, thou shalt fade ere noon.
What boots a life which in such haste forsakes thee?
Thou'rt wondrous frolic, being to die so soon,
And passing proud a little colour makes thee.

If thee thy brittle beauty so deceives,
Know then the thing that swells thee is thy bane;
For the same beauty doth, in bloody leaves,
The sentence of thy early death contain.

Some clown's coarse lungs will poison thy sweet flower,
If by the careless plough thou shalt be torn;
And many Herods lie in wait each hour
To murder thee as soon as thou art born—
Nay, force thy bud to blow—their tyrant breath
Anticipating life, to hasten death!

—Sir Richard Fanshawe.

Did you avoid the temptation to drop your voice on: soon, deceives, leaves, flower, hour, and breath? If you have made these mistakes you have obscured the meaning.

Who was Herod? Whom did he murder? How can a rose be murdered as soon as it is born? What does the word "anticipating" mean here? How can the life of a rose be "anticipated"?

Is there any connection between the word "Herod" and the word "tyrant"?

What characteristic of a "tyrant" is in the mind of the poet when he uses this word?

What idea about a rose is expressed in this poem?

Its beauty, far from being an advantage, is the cause of its early death.

Give other words for:

a. Boots, *b.* frolic, *c.* bane, *d.* bloody leaves.

Why is "bloody" a better adjective here than "crimson"? From where do the words "sentence", "tyrant", "murder" and "death" come? Is there any connection between the ideas they express? Now do you see why he chose that adjective?

What is a suspensory pause and why must you observe it?

How many strongly-stressed syllables are there in each line (verse) of this poem?

Would it (*a*) affect the rhythm? (*b*) alter the position of the strong beat if you were to substitute "red petals" for "bloody leaves"?

There are fourteen lines in this poem. There are five strong stresses in a line and each strong stress follows a weak one.

υ — υ — υ — υ — υ —

Notice, too, that the poem has a special rhyme scheme; work it out and you will find it is:

a b a b   c d c d   e f e f   gg.

This is the rhyme scheme of a Shakespearean sonnet.

These features of the poem, the number of lines, the arrangement of stresses, and of the rhyming words, are important because they help to make the pattern of the poem, but the length and shape of the vowel sounds, the sound of the consonants, the position of the pauses, the placing of the words that should be emphasized in the poem, are also important, for these contribute to the shape and pattern of the poem, and determine the rhythms.

Which are the words you would emphasize in this poem?

Remember that emphasis is the stressing of a word or words in a sentence in order to bring out the meaning.

7. "v" as in "vine."

V

"v"

Symbol: LOWER-CASE V
Phonemic classification: labio-dental voiced fricative
IPA usage: "vine"; "of"; "vivacious"
American English usage: same as IPA.

This is a voiced sound which follows the release of the contact of the upper teeth with the lower lip.

a. Exercises:

v v v	v v v	v v v	v
viv viv viv	viv viv viv	viv viv viv	viv
vav vav vav	vav vav vav	vav vav vav	vav
vuv vuv vuv	vuv vuv vuv	vuv vuv vuv	vuv
vov vov vov	vov vov vov	vov vov vov	vov
voov voov voov	voov voov voov	voov voov voov	voov
vivvety	vivvety	vivvity	viv
vovvity	vovvity	vovvity	vov
veevity	veevity	veevity	veev

b. Make a list of fifty words beginning with "v" and practice saying them, e.g., vine, voice, vinegar.
c. Make up nonsense rhymes that will afford exercise in attaining ability in the shaping of this sound.
d. Practice the following nonsense rhyme:

Evalina,
Evalina,
Did you ever see a cleaner
Little girl than Evalina?
Valda, Vernon, Vincent,
may be all dressed in white:
Veronica, it's possible,
may look a charming sight—
BUT
Never,
never,
Have I seen a
cleaner
Girl than Evalina

—D.L.

e. Practice aloud the following poem, using it not only to improve your way of articulating the "v" sound, but also to improve your power of expressing orally, in a simple, sincere and direct way, the thoughts and feelings it contains.

The Vagabond

Give to me the life I love,
Let the lave go by me,
Give the jolly heaven above
And the byway nigh me.
Bed in the bush with stars to see,
Bread I dip in the river—
There's the life for a man like me,
There's the life forever.

Let the blow fall soon or late,
Let what will be o'er me;
Give the face of earth around
And the road before me.
Wealth I seek not, hope nor love,
Nor a friend to know me;
All I seek, the heaven above
And the road below me.

Or let autumn fall on me
Where afield I linger,
Silencing the bird on tree,
Biting the blue finger.
White as meal the frosty field—
Warm the fireside haven—
Not to autumn will I yield,
Not to winter even!

Let the blow fall soon or late,
Let what will be o'er me;
Give the face of earth around,
And the road before me.
Wealth I ask not, hope nor love,
Nor a friend to know me;
All I ask, the heaven above
And the road below me.
—Robert Louis Stevenson.

Have you ever thought of the way in which the whole meaning of a sentence can be altered by changing the emphasis from one word to another?

Try to analyze the difference in meaning as a result of changing the emphasis from one word to another in the following sentence:

Are you going to the library today? The emphasis reveals impatience in the enquiry as to whether you are going or not going.

Are *you* going to the library today? Here the enquirer is concerned with whether you or someone else may be going.

Are you going to the *library* today? The placing of the emphasis on the word library suggests that the library may or may not be among the places at which you will call.

Are you going to the library *today*? Here the emphasis directs attention to the time of the visit.

Now look at *The Vagabond*, and make up your mind, by a series of experiments in the placing of the emphasis, which words should be emphasized if the meaning of the poet is to be made clear. The wrong placing of the emphasis can totally change the poet's meaning.

There are people who imagine that poetry is inaccurate, that it can mean whatever you think it means, but this is not true. A poet is a poet by reason of his power to use language with greater sensitiveness and accuracy than can the average person. He means exactly what he says, and though you may understand superficially the meaning of the words he uses you must, if you are to interpret him truthfully, understand fully the feelings he is expressing.

8. Soft "th" as in "thin"

θ

SOFT "TH"

Symbol: THETA
Phonemic classification: lingua-dental voiceless fricative
IPA usage: "thin"; "width"; "thousand"
American English usage: same as IPA.

When producing this sound, the tip of the tongue protrudes slightly between the upper and lower teeth and the sound is produced as the tongue tip is withdrawn from this position and the lower jaw moves down.

a. Exercises:

th th th	th th th	th th th	th
theth theth theth	theth theth theth	theth theth theth	theth
thith thith thith	thith thith thith	thith thith thith	thith
thuth thuth thuth	thuth thuth thuth	thuth thuth thuth	thuth
thoth thoth thoth	thoth thoth thoth	thoth thoth thoth	thoth

b. Make a list of words containing this sound, e.g., thin, thatch, thimble, thick, thread, width, thousand, breath.

c. Practice the following nonsense rhyme:

A thousand,
and a thousand, thousand years ago,
Living in the thickest jungle,
Was a snake called Flo.
She was coily, thick as thread,
From her tail to her head.

Queen Theresa Marrow-Bone,
Sitting, knitting on her throne,
Garments for the Princes three,
Exclaimed aloud—"Oh dearie me—
No more wool left for this scarf,
And I haven't finished half!"

Then the snake, whose name was Flo,
To the Queen courtesied low,
"How would you, your Majesty,
Like to knit with some of me?
I am coily, thin as thread,
And so pretty, too," she said.

So this snake, so very thin,
To the scarf was knitted in—
And protected well, I'm told—
Three small princes from the cold.
—D.L.

d. Practice the following poem aloud, paying particular attention to the distinction which exists between the voiced and the voiceless "th" sound.

Death, be not Proud

Death, be not proud, though some have called thee
Mighty and dreadful, for thou art not so:
For those whom thou think'st thou dost overthrow
Die not, poor Death, nor yet can'st thou kill me.

From rest and sleep, which but thy picture be,
Much pleasure, then from thee much more must flow
And soonest our best men with thee do go—
Rest of their bones and soul's delivery!

Thou'rt slave to fate, chance, kings, and desperate men,
And dost with poison, war, and sickness dwell;
And poppy or charms can make us sleep as well
And better than thy stroke, Why swellest thou then?
One short sleep past, we wake eternally,
And death shall be no more: Death, thou shalt die!
—John Donne.

About the Pattern of This Poem

Do you remember Richard Fanshawe's *A Rose*?

Like *Death, be not Proud,* it was a poem of fourteen lines (or verses) each one having five strong stresses and five weak stresses arranged thus:

∪ — ∪ — ∪ — ∪ — ∪ —

Such a verse is called an iambic pentameter. A poem of fourteen iambic pentameters is called a sonnet, so this must be a sonnet. Notice, however, that its rhyme scheme is not the same. "Thee" rhymes with "me", "be" and "delivery"; "so" with "overthrow", "flow" and "go". Thus the pattern is: a bb a. a bb a.

These eight lines form the octet of an Italian or Petrarchan sonnet and are followed by a sestet (six lines) rhyming: c d d c e e.

The rhyme scheme of the octet never varies, but the sestet can have a variety of rhymes, e.g., cd cd cd or c d e c d e.

You will notice that a sonnet has as its subject one central idea. Express in one sentence the central idea of the sonnet *Death, be not Proud.* In other words, what is it about? Does the poem express a belief in resurrection? Can you find a sentence in the poem that expresses a belief in the survival of personal identity?

With what does the poet compare death? How can "poppy" induce sleep? What does the poet mean by saying that death is "the slave of fate, chance, kings and desperate men"? Give an example of death being the slave of (*a*) chance, (*b*) kings, (*c*) desperate men.

Do you think that the poet takes a cheerful or gloomy view of life? Is he afraid of death? Do you think the poem expresses a very strong faith?

What word would you use to express the mood of this poem? Supply a word of your own choice or choose one from the following list:

Defiant, vindictive, sad, triumphant, confident, timid, angry, mournful, fearful, arrogant, buoyant, sentimental, loving.

This is a poem in which the placing of the emphasis, the stressing of the right words, can help to make clear both the meaning and the mood.

Here, too, a sensitive use of inflection can help to convey the meaning. "Mighty", for instance, does not mean the same as "dreadful". The sense of power expressed in the word "mighty" can be conveyed by the strong resonance in the initial "m" sound, and the inflection on the long vowel "i", together with the firm finish and precision of the "t" sound, but the word "dreadful" has the accompanying emotion of fear and this feeling should be conveyed in the way you say "dreadful". The sounds are abrupt and leaden. Go through this poem, paying particular attention to the inflection of vowel sounds. Notice the use of falling inflections on fate, chance, kings, men, and on poison, war and sickness, in the lines:

Thou'rt slave to fate, chance, kings, and desperate men,
And dost with poison, war and sickness dwell.

Why do you use these falling inflections, though the sentence is not complete? The answer is that you use falling inflections to keep separate ideas in a series.

This poem will give you a good deal of practice in the use of inflection for it has several enjambed verses where, though you use the suspensory pause, you must not use a falling inflection since the meaning is not complete, e.g., "thee" in line one, "overthrow" in line three, "well" in line eleven.

9. Hard "th" as in "them".

ð

HARD "TH"

Symbol: ETH
Phonemic classification: lingua-dental voiced fricative
IPA usage: "them"; "that"
American English usage: Same as IPA.

This sound is made by exactly the same movements of the tongue as the [θ] sound, except that the [ð] sound is a voiced consonant.

a. Exercises:

theth theth theth	theth theth theth
thith thith thith	thith thith thith
thuth thuth thuth	thuth thuth thuth
thoth thoth thoth	thoth thoth thoth
thath thath thath	thath thath thath
thooth thooth thooth	thooth thooth thooth
thawth thawth thawth	thawth thawth thawth
theeth theeth theeth	theeth theeth theeth

b. Make a list of fifty words containing this sound, e.g., with, this, that, then, those, whither, slither.

c. Practice the following nonsense rhyme:

Three little elves,
said to themselves:
"Let's tease,
these knees—
Let's pretend
we are fleas—
Let's slither and slide,
Hop,
skip,
then hide
When a voice murmurs—
"Fleas—
can you imagine it
FLEAS
on my knees?"
—D.L.

Practice the following poem, taking great care to distinguish between the voiced and voiceless "TH" sound.

Ode to Autumn

Season of mists and mellow fruitfulness,
Close bosom-friend of the maturing sun;
Conspiring with him how to load and bless
With fruit the vines that round the thatch-eaves run;
To bend with apples the moss'd cottage-trees,
And fill all fruit with ripeness to the core;
To swell the gourd, and plump the hazel shells
With a sweet kernel; to set budding more,
And still more, later flowers for the bees,
Until they think warm days will never cease;
For Summer has o'erbrimm'd their clammy cells.

Who hath not seen thee oft amid thy store?
Sometimes whoever seeks abroad may find
Thee sitting careless on a granary floor,
Thy hair soft-lifted by the winnowing wind;
Or on a half-reap'd furrow sound asleep,
Drows'd with the fume of poppies, while thy hook
Spares the next swath and all its twined flowers;
And sometimes like a gleaner thou dost keep
Steady thy laden head across a brook;
Or by a cider-press, with patient look,
Thou watchest the last oozings, hours by hours.

Where are the songs of Spring? Ay, where are they?
Think not of them,—thou hast thy music too,
While barrèd clouds bloom the soft-dying day
And touch the stubble-plains with rosy hue;
Then in wailful choir the small gnats mourn
Among the river sallows, borne aloft
Or sinking as the light wind lives or dies;
And full-grown lambs loud bleat from hilly bourn;
Hedge-crickets sing, and now with treble soft
The redbreast whistles from a garden-croft,
And gathering swallows twitter in the skies.

—*John Keats.*

In this poem Keats has described one of the seasons of the year. If the poem had no title how would you know that the poet was describing autumn? Choose six images which belong to autumn, or fall.

What occupations are mentioned in this poem? What sounds are associated with autumn in the mind of the poet? Which birds does he mention? If it had been springtime, which birds might he have mentioned? Why are the swallows "gathering"? Which picture in this poem most pleases you? Can you describe the atmosphere of this poem? If not, choose the word you consider most suitable from the following list:

Tranquil	Gay	Gloomy	Contended
Lethargic	Cheerful	Energetic	Peevish
Sombre	Serene	Calm	Sullen
Noisy	Restless	Passionate	Quiet

Does Keats describe a parched, arid, barren autumn, or a rich and fruitful one? Are his images drawn from the countryside and the farm, or from the town and the factory? Which of the poet's senses is most responsive in this poem? What time of the day does the poet especially describe? Is there any relation between the time of the day and the time of the year? Do you think it was by accident or design that he chose that time of the day? What does it add to the effect?

In this poem Keats has expressed his thoughts and feelings about fall. It is not only a description of a season of the year, but it is an expression of the mind of the poet, for he has made "a selection" from the innumerable experiences of this season of the year, and communicated them to us in such a way that we know what autumn meant for him. He makes us share his response to the richness and the beauty of Nature, because, while we read his word magic, we share his experience. That is the ultimate test of great poetry, that it not only says something to us, but that as we read we share the experience, and our lives are enriched.

Why should we want our lives to be enriched? If we could live through all the experiences in the world could we then do without poetry? The answer is "no". But why?

Do you think that perhaps it is because poetry, by making us share the vision of life of those who have greater awareness than ourselves, helps both to quicken and make more sensitive our own response to life, while at the same time it furnishes us with a means of comparing and contrasting many visions so that in the end we see and understand life more clearly?

There is a group of consonants known as the "lingua-palatal" or post-dental consonants, because the tongue tip and the teeth ridge behind the upper teeth are the organs of speech employed in their production.

Below is a list of such consonants:

[t] [d] [l] (clear)	[ɫ] (dark)	[n] [r] [ɹ]
[s] [z] [sh]	[zh]	[ch] [j]

There are thirteen altogether. It is interesting to think of all the experiments our ancestors must have made when they were trying to discover how many noises they could make by varying the movements of the tongue tip.

10. "t" as in "tap";

t

"T"

Symbol: LOWER-CASE T
Phonemic classification: lingua-alveolar voiceless stop-plosive
IPA usage: "tap"; "sitting"
American English usage: Same as IPA

The tongue tip is in contact with the teeth ridge behind the upper teeth, and the sound follows the release of this contact.

a. Practice the following:

tat tat tat	tat tat tat	tat tat tat	tat
tet tet tet	tet tet tet	tet tet tet	tet
tot tot tot	tot tot tot	tot tot tot	tot

tut tut tut	tut tut tut	tut tut tut	tut
tawt tawt tawt	tawt tawt tawt	tawt tawt tawt	tawt
toht toht toht	toht toht toht	toht toht toht	toht
toot toot toot	toot toot toot	toot toot toot	toot
tite tite tite	tite tite tite	tite tite tite	tite
tettity	tettity	tettity	tet
tattity	tattity	tattity	tat
tottity	tottity	tottity	tot
tawtity	tawtity	tawtity	tawt

b. Make a list of fifty words with the initial "t" sound, e.g., topple, toes, test.
c. Use some of the words in composing nonsense verses which will afford practice in shaping these sounds, e.g.:

Tientsein was a tadpole,
A real Tibetan tadpole,
Quite the most Tibetan tadpole in Tibet.

The Tibetans thought him holy—
Called the tiny tadpole holy—
and fed him on the meat,
Of tarantula, and sweet:
Toffee, treacle toffee—
Quite the sweetest treacle toffee,
They could get,
In ALL Tibet.

What a lucky, lucky tadpole,
Was this real Tibetan tadpole:
With the tall Tibetan mountains,
Stretching peaks into the sky—
Do you know why?
These mountains stretched their peaks,
For weeks and weeks and weeks,
To the sky, and the beyond?
To protect this little tadpole
This tiny, tiny tadpole,
in his pond.

—D.L.

Remember that the distinctness of your speech depends largely on the neatness and firmness of the contact of the organs of speech used in shaping the consonants. Open your mouth well, and use the tip of the tongue to shape the "t" sound. Finish off the final consonant in every word.

d. Practice saying the following sonnet aloud:

Sonnet

Like as the waves make towards the pebbled shore,
So do our minutes hasten to their end;
Each changing place with that which goes before,
In sequent toil all forwards do contend.

Nativity, once in the main of light,
Crawls to maturity, wherewith being crown'd
Crooked eclipses 'gainst his glory fight,
And Time that gave doth now his gift confound.

Time doth transfix the flourish set on youth
And delves the parallels in beauty's brow,
Feeds on the rarities of nature's truth,
And nothing stands but for his scythe to mow:

And yet to times in hope my verse shall stand,
Praising they worth, despite his cruel hand.
—*William Shakespeare.*

Having worked on this sonnet for speech practice and especially for the improvement of the consonant "t", you should then ask yourself what the poem is about.

The poet is stating his conviction that art alone escapes the destructive power of time. He claims that life passes swiftly and relentlessly from birth to maturity and so to death. Youth and beauty cannot resist the ravages of time, but this poem, in which he celebrates the beauty of his friend, will be immortal.

To express his ideas Shakespeare has chosen certain images. For instance, the minutes that compose our lives are likened to the waves that succeed one another on the shore.

What aspect of the waves is in the mind of the poet? It is not their wetness, not their color, not their power, but their movement. Each wave is succeeded by another, and no power that we can exert can alter this. Similarly, the stages of our life's development are compared with the journey of the sun from dawn to high noon, and from high noon to set of sun. Why is this a good comparison?

Of what is the poet thinking? Not the color of the sun nor its path, but of how it becomes stronger and more powerful as the day waxes towards noon, and of how it grows weaker and less powerful until it wanes altogether at the end of the day.

With this idea others are associated. The rising sun gives promise of a glorious day. Growth, activity, achievement, belong normally to the daylight hours. And as you think about this image of the sun, and why it is so well-suited to the poet's purpose, write down all the associated ideas that come into your mind. Thus you will train your power of visualizing, of seeing the pictures the words make. It is a way of developing your imagination, and it is very important that you should develop this power.

Time doth transfix the flourish set on youth
And delves the parallels in beauty's brow.

The "parallels in beauty's brow" are wrinkles. These are a sign of age and of care. A beautiful and youthful brow is smooth. Thought and physical strain are registered in these wrinkles. Look at the words "delves the parallels". The word "delves" belongs to agriculture. It suggests labor in the fields in the attempt to produce corn—the means of subsistence. The word "parallels" belongs to a form of intense mental activity—mathematics. Thus, by the use of these two words "delves" and "parallels" the poet skilfully suggests the ways in which wrinkles have been induced—by physical exertion and mental strain.

There are some people who think that the words a poet uses are merely accidental. Nothing could be farther from the truth. A poet cares tremendously about the accurate use of language, and if you are to have a mind that is clear and vital, you, too, must learn to understand the implications of the way in which you have used words. To do this you must see the pictures that the words make, and encourage your mind to think of the ideas associated with each word.

You cannot hope to be a good speaker until you have trained yourself to see the pictures words make, for the tones of your voice, the subtlety of your expression, depend on your power to visualize fully the meaning of what you are saying. Perfect expression in speech is the result of a long training in visualizing meaning, and controlling your breathing, your enunciation, your articulation, and the inflections and modulations, etc., of your voice. These are inter-dependent. They are the physical and intellectual aspects of speech, and they are just as dependent on each other as are your body and your brain.

11. "d" as in "daddy".

d

"D"

Symbol: LOWER-CASE D
Phonemic classification: lingua-alveolar voiced stop-plosive
IPA usage: "daddy"
American English usage: Same as IPA.

[d] is a voiced plosive consonant. If follows the release of the tongue tip from the ridge behind the upper teeth.

a. Exercises for [d]:

d d d	d d d	d d d	d
dad dad dad	dad dad dad	dad dad dad	dad
ded ded ded	ded ded ded	ded ded ded	ded
did did did	did did did	did did did	did

dod dod dod	dod dod dod	dod dod dod	dod
dud dud dud	dud dud dud	dud dud dud	dud
daddidy	daddidy	daddidy	dad
doddedy	doddedy	doddedy	dod
duddety	duddety	duddety	dud
diddety	diddety	diddety	did

b. Make a list of fifty words with the initial [d] sound, e.g., dance, devotion, duty.
c. Use some of these words in composing nonsense verses which will give you practice in saying this sound, e.g.:

Doreen Dahlia was definitely devoted,
To a debonair dandelion,
and it was noted—
By the daisy and the daffodil,
That Doreen was becoming ill—
so ill,
and moaning, "I'm a dreadful failure:
I'm a dreadful, dreadful failure,"
sobbed devoted Doreen Dahlia.
"For my darling Dandelion,
so dashing and so debonair,
Has departed from my life,
with a naughty puff of air!"
—*D.L.*

d. Practice saying the following poem. It not only affords you practice in the shaping of the consonant "d" but it makes great demands on your breath control. See what you can do with it.

The Windhover (to Christ Our Lord)

I caught this morning morning's minion, kingdom of daylight's
dauphin, dapple-dawn-drawn Falcon, in his riding
Of the rolling level underneath him steady air, and striding
High there, how he rung upon the rein of a wimpling wing
In his ecstasy! then off, off forth on swing,
As a skate's heel sweeps smooth on a bow bend; the hurl and
gliding
Rebuffed the big wind. My heart in hiding
Stirred for a bird—the achieve of, the mastery of the thing!
Brute beauty and valour and act, oh, air, pride, plume, here
Buckle! and the fire that breaks from thee then, a billion
Times told lovelier, more dangerous, O my chevalier!
No wonder of it: sheer plod makes plough down sillion
Shine, and blue-black embers, ah my dear,
Fall, gall themselves, and gash gold-vermilion.
—*Gerard Manley Hopkins.*

The author of this poem once advised a friend who said he could not understand his poems to take a deep breath and say them aloud. No poet has ever more fully realized than did Gerard Manley Hopkins that the printed word is merely the photograph of speech, and that if you want fully to grasp the living reality of words you must speak them aloud.

This poem is a description of a hunting bird in flight, but it is more than that. It is the expression of the thoughts and feelings of a man who not only admired the control of its medium which the bird demonstrated, but shared the bird's enjoyment of the exercise of that power. As he watches, other thoughts come to him, and he realizes that it is no wonder that he should be thrilled by the falcon's achievement of a complete mastery and control of its world, a world dangerous to it, but for its skill, and perfect physical control, for beauty is to be found wherever energy is released, in dying embers, which suddenly gash gold vermilion, and light, and in the intense electric blues and greens and purples reflected in the smooth cut on heavy clay, made by the sharp pressure of a wheel.

How would you know that this poet has (i) very observant eyes; (ii) great intensity of feeling?

Practice saying this poem until you can convey all the sensitiveness in response, and the intensity of feeling which the poet has expressed in this poem. Why does he address this poem to Christ Our Lord?

Do you think he sees any connection between the conflict and the mastery of the bird on a physical level, and the conflict and the striving of man for mastery on the spiritual level?

Riding Rein Pride Plume Buckle Chevalier	All these ideas are associated with knighthood and chivalry, which was the medieval expression of the idealism and aspiration of the finest men of the Middle Ages.

Medieval chivalry was a cult in which the physical, the mental and the spiritual aspects of being were disciplined in the pursuit of perfection.

This is not an easy, but a rewarding, poem to work upon.

Now let us think of the problems that this poem presents to the speaker.

If it is not properly phrased the meaning cannot be conveyed. There are a great many or run-on, lines in this poem, and the phrases are sometimes so lengthy that to speak them well makes great demands on the speaker's breath control.

I caught this morning —· morning's minion — King-
dom of daylight's Dauphin —· dapple-dawn-drawn
Falcon —
in his riding/
Of the rolling level —· underneath him
steady air —· and striding/

High there —· how he rung upon the
rein of the wimpling wing — /
In his ecstasy —

Above, the phrases are marked with a dash (—), the suspensory pauses with a stroke (/), and the places where you should replenish your breath with a (·). Notice that though you can never replenish your breath except at a pause, yet you cannot do so even there on all occasions. There are only five pauses at which the breath can be replenished. For instance, it would be fatal to replenish your breath at any of the suspensory pauses. These are so brief that any break in the continuity would destroy the meaning.

Notice, also, what demands this poem makes on your control of falling inflections. It is only when you come to the word ecstasy that you can use a falling inflection. The meaning overflows every one of the first four verses, i.e., the poem is full of run-on lines, and you must be careful not to use falling inflections on "daylight's", "riding", "striding", "wing". If you are to succeed you must have adequate breath control, for failing breath and falling inflections tend to go together.

Nor is it only the phrasing of this poem that will make demands on your breathing. Look at those long vowels:

I caught this morning morning's minion, kingdom of daylight's Dauphin.

Seven long vowel sounds in fifteen syllables. And look at those plosive consonants—"k" and "d" making great demands on energy, for they are there to express energy, and, last of all, look at the liquid consonants "m" and "ng", "l" and "r" and "n". Everyone of the liquid consonants is in the first two verses—twenty-four in the two verses. They are there to re-echo the sense of the passage—power and smoothness as well as energy are reflected in the bird's flight, and therefore the poet has expressed them in the movement and sweep of the language he uses to describe these things.

12. "n" as in "n̲ose."

n

"N"

Symbol: LOWER-CASE N

Phonemic classification: lingua-alveolar voiced nasal

IPA usage: "n̲ose"; "p̲n̲eumatic"; "k̲n̲ee"

American English usage: same as IPA.

Here we have another nasal consonant, for in the production of this consonant the sound, as in the case of [m], flows through the nose. It cannot get out through the mouth since the tongue tip is in close contact with the teeth ridge behind the upper teeth.

When you practice this sound make an effort to increase the resonance you employ in its production.

Remember what you have learned about:

1. The abdominal press.
2. Relaxing the lower jaw.

a. Exercises:

n n n	n n n	n n n	n
non non non	non non non	non non non	non
nin nin nin	nin nin nin	nin nin nin	nin
nun nun nun	nun nun nun	nun nun nun	nun
nen nen nen	nen nen nen	nen nen nen	nen
ninnie	ninnie	ninnie	ninnie
ninnity nin	ninnity nin	ninnity nin	
nonnety non	nonnety non	nonnety non	
nunnity nun	nunnity nun	nunnity nun	

b. Make a list of fifty words with this "n" sound, e.g., now, gnarl, wooden, incredible, never, gnat, golden, innocent, nod, knob, sudden, inventory, noise, knack, endless, sun.

c. Use some of the words in composing nonsense rhymes, which will afford you practice in shaping this sound.

Non
Non
Ninnity-Nin,
Was a golden safety-pin,
specially knighted
Sir Non Non,
For services rendered in staying upon—
(In spite of incredible,
endless wind,)
and never forgetting
he was pinned
By his head, and by his knuckle,
In the centre of one green buckle!

—D.L.

d. Say the following poem:

A Thing of Beauty

A thing of beauty is a joy for ever:
Its loveliness increases; it will never
Pass into nothingness; but still will keep
A bower quiet for us, and a sleep
Full of quiet dreams, and health, and quiet breathing.
Therefore, on every morrow, are we wreathing
A flowery band to bind us to the earth,

Spite of despondence, of the inhuman dearth
Of noble natures, of the gloomy days,
Of all the unhealthy and o'er-darken'd ways
Made for our searching: yes, in spite of all,
Some shape of beauty moves away the pall
From our dark spirits. Such the sun, the moon,
Trees old and young, sprouting a shady boon
For simple sheep; and such are daffodils
With the green world they live in; and clear rills
That for themselves a cooling covert make
'Gainst the hot season; the mid-forest brake,
Rich with a sprinkling of fair musk-rose blooms;
And such too is the grandeur of the dooms
We have imagined for the mighty dead;
All lovely tales that we have heard or read:
An endless fountain of immortal drink,
Pouring unto us from the heaven's brink.

Nor do we merely feel these essences
For one short hour: no, even as the trees
That whisper round a temple become soon
Dear as the temple's self, so does the moon,
The passion poesy, glories infinite,
Haunt us till they become a cheering light
Unto our souls, and bound to us so fast,
That, whether there be shine, or gloom, o'ercast,
They always must be with us, or we die.

—*John Keats.*

Here is a poem of direct statement. "A thing of beauty is a joy forever." The poet goes on to express his conviction that beauty has a great influence on our physical and spiritual health. Squalor and dirt and disorder depress us, and if we allow these things to continue until we are so blunted in response that we no longer notice them, this process in which the senses are blunted will be reflected in our physical being. If you were to read Dickens' *Bleak House* you would find plenty of evidence that he thought so, too.

Keats, in this poem, tells us of the things which he thought beautiful. The sun, the moon, the stars—daffodils, with the green world they live in.

You will notice that many of these things are natural objects which appeal to the sense of sight, or the sense of sound, but these are not the only source of beauty. There is the beauty of human action—of those who "in their lives fought for life". They are the "mighty dead", the grandeur of whose dooms is still a source of inspiration to the human race.

Can you give the names of six such people? Tell briefly the stories of such heroic lives. Where else does Keats find beauty apart from the beauty of nature and the beauty of human action and suffering? He finds it in literature. Try to remember one "lovely tale" that you have heard or read.

Keats was a wonderful teller of tales. You should read either his *Eve of St. Agnes* or *The Pot of Basil.*

Samuel Taylor Coleridge tells the lovely tale of the Ancient Mariner. Have you read it? If you know no lovely tales then it is time that you "furnished that room" in your mind. Go and read!

What form of literature does Keats single out for special praise? What does he mean by "the glories infinite" of poetry?

This is perhaps the time to begin to think about the qualities of poetry for which men value it, and which distinguish it from prose.

Discuss with other people their ideas on the characteristics of poetry and the use of poetry.

Write down your ideas on the subject. Collect evidence in support of those ideas.

One day you may be called upon to support, or oppose the assertion: "As civilization advances, poetry must necessarily decay."

What is your opinion on the subject?

13. "l" as in "clear."

l

CLEAR "L"

Symbol: LOWER-CASE L
Phonemic classification: lingua-alveolar voiced lateral
IPA usage: "clear"
American English usage: same as IPA.

The letter "l" stands for two quite different sounds, distinguished in phonetics by the use of the following symbols: [l] (clear), [ɫ] (dark).

a. Clear [l] is the sound used before vowels, as in the words: clear, liquid, lost. The tongue tip is in contact with the upper teeth ridge, and the blade of the tongue is tensed and lifted towards the palate. The sound flows over the edges of the tongue and can be prolonged, as is the case with the other liquid consonants: m, n, ng and r. Consonants which can be prolonged at will are called continuants.
b. Practice saying the following words aloud:

lever	lentil	ladle	lost
light	lion	lotion	blear
live	libel	loyal	cloister
line	lively	loiter	clear
like	lonely	local	clatter
lovely	liquid	languid	lazy

c. Exercises:

l l l	l l l	l l l	l
lil lil lil	lil lil lil	lil lil lil	lil
lol lol lol	lol lol lol	lol lol lol	lol
lul lul lul	lul lul lul	lul lul lul	lul
lel lel lel	lel lel lel	lel lel lel	lel
lohl lohl lohl	lohl lohl lohl	lohl lohl lohl	lohl

d. Practice the following rhyme:

Lionel was a Lollipop,
and
Lionel was a waiter;
Lionel used to carry meals
To an alligator:

Luscious, lovely, lumptious meals,
Boiled Cod,
and Jellied Eels,
Lion manes
and Lion claws,
Mixed in lightly with the paws
And liver of an ancient Llama,
All the way from Yokohama.

What a lucky Lollipop—
Couldn't even wait or stop,
To let me lick his pretty head—
"Like my job too much,"
he said!

—D.L.

e. In practicing the poem below pay particular attention to the "l" sound wherever it occurs. Hold it, lengthen it, and be sure that your mouth is open wide enough to allow your tongue sufficient freedom of movement to shape this sound firmly and neatly:

Morning Express

Along the wind-swept platform, pinched and white,
The travellers stand in pools of wintry light,
Offering themselves to morn's long, slanting arrows,
The train's due; porters trundle laden barrows.
The train steams in, volleying resplendent clouds
Of sun-blown vapour. Hither and about,
Scared people hurry, storming the doors in crowds.
The officials seem to waken with a shout,

Resolved to hoist and plunder; some to the vans
Leap; others rumble the milk in gleaming cans.
Boys, indolent-eyed, from baskets leaning back,
Question each face; a man with a hammer steals
Stooping from coach to coach; with clang and clack,
Touches and tests, and listens to the wheels.
Guard sounds a warning whistle, points to the clock
With brandished flag, and on his folded flock
Claps the last door: the monster groans: "Enough!"
Tightening his load of links with pant and puff.
Under the arch, then forth into blue day,
Glide the processional windows on their way,
And glimpse the stately folk who sit at ease
To view the world like kings taking the seas
In prosperous weather: drifting banners tell
Their progress to the counties; with them goes
The clamour of their journeying; while those
Who sped them stand to wave a last farewell.

—Siegfried Sassoon.

Morning Express is a useful poem for practice in finishing final consonants and for exercise in breath control, for the phrasing makes demands on good breath control. It also affords good training in imagination. You must see all the pictures noticed by the poet and make the listener see them as you say them.

Now is the time to think of another very important aspect of interpretation. Too often when people memorize the printed word they speak at an even pace. Natural speech is never even paced. Thoughts move in the mind at an uneven pace. Think about this when you say *Morning Express.* Notice how the poem begins. The pace is slow, then the excitement quickens as the train is about to arrive, and there is a change in pace as "scared people" and officials hurry about. Look at that phrase "scared people". Why are they scared? Not because they may fall over a precipice, or drown, but because they are suddenly aware of the possibility of missing the train. It makes them anxious. It hurries their steps and it brings into their minds all the worries that would accumulate if they did not catch the train. Think of the many reasons these people have for wanting to catch the train. Some are going on a vacation. Seas and mountains, rivers and forests beckon. Pleasure lies ahead. Some are going to offices for the routine of a day's work. Some may be going to interviews which will take them to the ends of the earth, or simply to their daily place of work. Some are bent on a day's shopping, and one perhaps is to consult a doctor, or has been called to the side of a relative injured in an accident. There are all sorts of reasons for not missing that train, and these possibilities must be in your mind or you will use the wrong inflections on the word "scared".

Visualize the "pools of wintery light". Why does the poet use the word "pools"? What is in his mind? Why does the light fall in pools? What are the drifting banners? Why is the word "drifting" appropriate? Is there any association of ideas in using the word "banners" and the image "like kings takings the seas" in prosperous weather? What is prosperous weather? Why should kings take the seas? Can you think of any kings who have done so?

From what source has the poet derived these images? What effect do these images have in creating atmosphere?

Is the final impression that the poem makes on you cheerful or gloomy?

14. "L" as in "dull."

ɫ

DARK "L"

Symbol: TILDE L
Phonemic classification: velarized lingua alveolar voiced lateral
IPA usage: used after postvocalic laterals "all "; "bell ", "hill "
American English usage: same as IPA

Dark "l", which in phonetics is written [ɫ], is the sound which occurs after vowel sounds. As in the case of clear [l], the tongue tip is in contact with the teeth ridge, and the sound flows over the edges of the tongue. It is for this reason called a lateral consonant. But notice the state of the tongue. In dark "l" the tongue is not tensed but lax. It curves towards the lower jaw, instead of away from the lower jaw as in clear "l". The lower jaw is slightly more relaxed and open than in the case of clear "l". This is a sound of which you must be very careful because all vowel sounds used in combination with it tend to be blunted and to lose their individual quality and fineness. This is especially the case with short "i" and short "e".

a. Exercises:

bill bill bill	bill bill bill	bill bill bill	bill
boll boll boll	boll boll boll	boll boll boll	boll
ball ball ball	ball ball ball	ball ball ball	ball
bull bull bull	bull bull bull	bull bull bull	bull
bell bell bell	bell bell bell	bell bell bell	bell

Prolong the final "l" to the extent that your breath control will allow you, and listen always to the effect it is having on the preceding vowel.

b. Practice saying the following words:

elf	wealth	silk	twelfth	grill
shelf	health	milk	twill	hill
delf	stealth	wilk	bill	mill

c. Use some of these words in composing nonsense rhymes, which will afford practice in shaping these sounds, e.g.:

Twelve elves,
helped themselves—
To twelve jars
on some shelves.
"Oh lovely Lollipops"
the elder elf,
said "Upon my shelf."

"I've found a lemon and a lime"
Elf eleven said "in mine."
BUT
Baby elf cried aloud,
and stamped his feet—
"In this jar of mine",
he said—
"There's nothing I can eat".

"There's the beak of an albatross—
and
A piece of glossy slime"—
"What a shame",
said the elf—
"What a shame—
to steal a jar like mine!"

—D.L.

d. *The Shell* is a poem which will give you practice in the use of this sound. Practice saying the poem aloud, bearing in mind the dark "l" sound. Try to make up your mind about the effect of the repeated use of the [ɫ] sound.

The Shell

And then I pressed the shell
Close to my ear
And listened well,
And straightway like a bell
Came low and clear
The slow sad murmur of far distant seas,
Whipped by an icy breeze
Upon a shore
Wind-swept and desolate.
It was a sunless strand that never bore
The footprint of a man,
Nor felt the weight
Since time began
Of any human quality or stir

Save what the dreary winds and waves incur.
And in the hush of waters was the sound
Of pebbles rolling round,
For ever rolling with a hollow sound.
And bubbling seaweeds as the waters go
Swish to and fro
Their long, cold tentacles of shiny grey.
There was no day,
Nor ever came a night
Setting the stars alight
To wonder at the moon:
Twas twilight only and the frightened croon,
Smitten to whimpers, of the dreary wind
And waves that journeyed blind—
And then I loosed my ear—O, it was sweet
To hear a cart go jolting shown the street!
—James Stephens.

The whole poem is a word picture, in which the atmosphere is very important. Try to find out how the poet achieves this atmosphere. He does it by suggesting appropriate images to our mind's eye, e.g., distant seas—icy breeze—a shore, windswept and desolate. He stresses the absence of human beings. Find the phrases in which he does this.

Not only does he appeal to the eye, but to the ear: "The hush of water: for ever rolling with a hollow sound—frightened croon—smitten to whimpers."

Morning Express and *The Shell* are both word pictures, in which the creation of mood and atmosphere play a great part. Notice the movement in both poems. *Morning Express* is brisk compared with *The Shell,* for the ideas are briefly and tersely expressed and there are many of them. The rhythms of *The Shell* are slow moving except for occasional eddies. This is achieved in many ways.

First of all, notice the length of the sentences. Notice how many run-on lines there are, and, therefore, from the point of view of the speaker, how many temptations which must be avoided, to use a falling inflection with the suspensory pause. Notice, too, the variation in the position, and the number of stresses in each verse (line). All these give width and variety to the rhythm, but its slow movement is achieved, too, by the use of long vowels and sonorous consonants, especially the dark [ɫ] and the liquid m, n and ng.

This is a poem in which sound echoes the sense. From being held in the grip of a weird and terrifying enchantment the listener is suddenly freed and back in the cheerful light of the everyday world, and relieved to be there. Brisk and cheerful are the sounds of the plosives that express the thought and feeling of relief: *to hear* a cart go jolting down the street.

Make no mistake. Such things are not accidents. They are the product of a perfect integration of thought and feeling, expressed in speech which is the "body" of these things.

e. *Real Property* will give you further opportunity to appreciate the quality of the dark [ɫ] sound.

Real Property

Tell me about that harvest field.
Oh! Fifty acres of living bread.
The colour has painted itself in my heart.
The form is patterned in my head.

So now I take it everywhere;
See it whenever I look around;
Hear it growing through every sound,
Know exactly the sound it makes—
Remembering, as one must all day,
Under the pavement the live earth aches.

Trees are at the farther end,
Limes all full of the mumbling bee:
So there must be a harvest field
Whenever one thinks of a linden tree.

A hedge is about it, very tall,
Hazy and cool, and breathing sweet.
Round paradise is such a wall
And all the day, in such a way,
In paradise the wild birds call.

You only need to close your eyes
And go within your secret mind,
And you'll be into paradise:
I've learn quite easily to find
Some linden trees and drowsy bees,
A tall sweet hedge with the corn behind.

I will not have that harvest mown:
I'll keep the corn and leave the bread.
I've bought that field; it's now my own;
I've fifty acres in my head
I take it as a dream to bed,
I carry it about all day. . . .

Sometimes when I have found a friend
I give a blade of corn away.
—Harold Munro.

15a. "r" as in "ran."

r

ROLLED R

Symbol: LOWER-CASE R
Phonemic classification: lingua-velar glide (semi-vowel)
IPA usage: "ran"
American English usage: same as IPA.
American English usage: same as IPA, if used.

This sound is made by a series of rapid taps of the tongue tip against the teeth ridge. It occurs only before vowel sounds, e.g., river, reed, wren, through, thrust, thrive.

15b. "r" as in "heart"

ɹ

SMOOTH R

Symbol: TURNED R
Phonemic classification: Voiced alveolar or postalveolar approximant
IPA usage: "heart", "harm"
American English usage: same as IPA if used

After vowel sounds the consonant used is not the trilled (or rolled) [r] but the smooth "r" [ɹ], which consists of one tap of the tongue tip against the teeth ridge, e.g., arm, harm, heart; *not* arum, harum, hearut.

a. Exercises:

r r r	r r r	r r r	r
rip rip rip	rip rip rip	rip rip rip	rip
rap rap rap	rap rap rap	rap rap rap	rap
rup rup rup	rup rup rup	rup rup rup	rup
rohp rohp rohp	rohp rohp rohp	rohp rohp rohp	rohp
rawr rawr rawr	rawr rawr rawr	rawr rawr rawr	rawr
rippety	rippety	rippety	rip
roppety	roppety	roppety	rop
ruppety	ruppety	ruppety	rup

b. Make two lists of words, the first containing examples of the rolled "r" and the second containing examples of the smooth "r", e.g., rack, roast, rent; darn, earn, hurt.

c. The following nonsense rhyme will afford exercise in the shaping of the rolled "r":

I saw a reed,
a wren,
a river:

I saw a mushroom stalk a-quiver.
I saw a grain of corn
a-rusting—
I saw a rivet's head a-thrusting
through the ground:
I watched a farmer,
reaping rain—
Whilst all around fell red-hot grain;
I watched a rip-rap-roppety ratchet,
Rush in terror from a hatchet—
I saw—
but then my mother spoke,
And with a sigh,
I a-woke,
Left wondering, if a ratchet bled,
If it was hit upon the head.

—D.L

d. A common mistake made by speakers is to insert an "r" between two vowels where it does not belong. This is called "bridging the hiatus". It is a "speech crime", e.g., the law (r) of the land, the India (r) of the eighteenth century, I saw (r) a mouse.

Eliminate the bracketed "r" when you are saying those sentences. If you have difficulty, practice the following vowel sound combinations:

aw—a	aw—a	aw—a	aw—a
(ɔ—æ)	(ɔ—æ)	(ɔ—æ)	(ɔ—æ)
a—o	a—o	a—o	a—o
(æ—ɒ)	(æ—ɒ)	(æ—ɒ)	(æ—ɒ)

e. Here is a nonsense rhyme which will give you further practice:

"I do declare,"
Said the bear—
"I'm alarmed:
There should be a law,
passed before,
Any harm is done,
to anyone.
Arum lilies,
the sillies—
Insist on growing,
in rivers,
fully knowing,
That bees,
seeking honey in these

Lilies,
dive down—
Their trumpets—
and drown!"
—*D.L.*

f. The following poems will afford you further practice in saying trilled and smooth "r" sounds:

Tartary

If I were Lord of Tartary,
Myself, and me alone,
My bed should be of ivory,
Of beaten gold my throne;
And in my court should peacocks flaunt,
And in my forests tigers haunt,
And in my pools great fishes slant
Their fins athwart the sun.

If I were Lord of Tartary,
Trumpeters every day
To all my meals should summon me,
And in my courtyards bray;
And in the evening lamps should shine,
Yellow as honey, red as wine,
While harp, and flute, and mandoline
Made music sweet and gay.

If I were Lord of Tartary,
I'd wear a robe of beads,
White, and gold, and green they'd be—
And small and thick as seeds;
And ere should wane the morning star,
I'd don my robe and scimitar,
And zebras seven should draw my car
Through Tartary's dark glades.

Lord of the fruits of Tartary,
Her rivers silver-pale!
Lord of the hills of Tartary,
Glen, thicket, wood and dale!
Her flashing stars, her scented breeze,
Her trembling lakes, like foamless seas,
Her bird-delighting citron-trees,
In every purple vale!
—*Walter de la Mare.*

Look at the title *Tartary*. Why is it a suitable one? Where is Tartary? What comes into your mind when you see or say the word? Can you find a word that expresses the difference between this land and America?

The poem is full of pictures of living things. Peacocks, tigers, great fishes, zebras, birds. Where are these things to be found? What other images would help you to place Tartary if you did not know where it was?

Choose images that suggest to you the splendor of an oriental court. Can you find a "barbaric touch" in the splendor of this court? Find an image that suggests danger, and fierceness, and cruelty? From what associations with the word "scimitar" do you derive this impression of a picture exotic and colorful? Can you suggest how the poet achieves this impression? Is the appeal of *Tartary* to the sense of sight alone? Do you consider this a romantic or a realistic picture of Tartary? What do you mean by romantic? And realistic?

The following poem *La Belle Dame Sans Merci* was chosen for many reasons. It will, of course, provide you with practice in the use of the smooth [r] sound, but it is also an excellent contrast in many ways to *Tartary*. They are both "romantic" in the treatment of the theme. But *Tartary* is a purely descriptive lyric, whereas Keats' poem, in spite of the lyrical quality of its descriptions, unfolds a story.

La Belle Dame Sans Merci

"O what can ail thee, knight-at-arms,
Alone and palely loitering?
The sedge is wither'd from the lake,
And no birds sing.

"O what can ail thee, knight-at-arms,
So haggard and so woe-begone?
The squirrel's granary is full,
And the harvest's done.

I see a lily on thy brow
With anguish moist and fever dew;
And on thy cheek a fading rose
Fast withereth too."

"I met a lady in the meads,
Full beautiful, a faery's child,
Her hair was long, her foot was light,
And her eyes were wild.

"I made a garland for her head,
And bracelets too, and fragrant zone;
She look'd at me as she did love
And made sweet moan.

"I set her on my pacing steed
And nothing else saw all day long,
For sideways would she lean and sing,
A faery's song.

"She found me roots of relish sweet,
And honey wild and manna dew,
And sure in language strange she said,
'I love thee true!'

"She took me to her elfin grot,
And there she wept and sigh'd full sore;
And there I shut her wild, wild eyes,
With kisses four.

"And there she lulléd me asleep,
And there I dream'd—ah! woe betide!
The latest dream I ever dream'd
On the cold hill's side.

"I saw pale kings and princes too
Pale warriors, death pale were they all;
Who cried, 'La belle Dame san Merci
Hath thee in thrall!'

"I saw their starved lips in the gloom
With horrid warning gapéd wide,
And I awoke and found me here
On the cold hill's side.

"And this is why I sojourn here
Alone and palely loitering,
Though the sedge is wither'd from the lake,
And no birds sing."

—John Keats.

This is one of the lovely tales that Keats told, and you might regard it simply as a poem of direct statement. It is the story of a knight who is beguiled and betrayed by the beautiful merciless lady to whom he devoted his life. But perhaps the whole story is an allegorical way of expressing something else, and then everything that happens in the poem stands for something not expressed, but implied or symbolized. What if *La Belle Dame Sans Merci* is another name for Life? What if the knight is Everyman who devotes himself to the service of some cause, or the attainment of some ideal, and in the end finds himself worn out and no nearer the achievement of the goal?

As we live our lives, absorbed in what we pursue, we are apt to forget all the other members of the human race, who have sacrificed themselves to the same ideal or the same cause. Notice how absorbed the knight is in his experience, "and nothing else saw all the day".

That is what happens to us in life, absorbed in "a single purpose", enchanted and beguiled in the pursuit of it, we do not notice the passage of time as we listen to "the faery's song".

Take the stanza:

"She found me roots of relish sweet,
And honey wild and manna dew,
And sure in language strange she said,
'I love thee true!' "

This stanza is easy to understand as "direct statement", but try to discover its "oblique" or "symbolic" meaning.

"Relish sweet" is surely a description of food that is refreshing and pleasing to the palate. In what experiences have you found refreshment and pleasure for your mind and spirit? Each human being will answer this differently. What is your answer? It all depends on where your interests lie.

Look at these two phrases— "honey wild" and "manna dew". Both of these are associated with experiences recorded in the Bible. Can you remember them? If not, read the story of John the Baptist and the story of the Israelites, when, coming out of Egypt, they sought the land of Canaan. "Honey wild and manna dew" were life, as well as physical refreshment for people who had embarked on a great and dangerous spiritual adventure—John the Baptist in the wilderness and the Israelites in the desert. For those who embark on the adventure of living, "the food of the spirit" is to be found in strange and unexpected forms and places, and you cannot know ahead of time what this will be, or where it will be found.

Do you begin to see how rich in association is Keats' choice of words? Do you remember that he talked of "loading every rift with ore"? Great poetry is always full of allusions. It makes demands on your experience of life and your knowledge. It stimulates you to wander in strange seas of thought, and the reward is an enrichment of your own vision of life.

If you were the knight would you rather have, or forgo, the experience? What effect does the poet achieve by associating the adventure with kings and princes? Do you think, perhaps, that he thought the nobleness of life merited this? What are great spiritual adventures on which men have embarked? Try to name some of these.

Think of the adventure of Columbus, of Galileo, of Madame Curie, of Christ, of Florence Nightingale. What had they in common?

Do you think it was to make truth prevail?

As you begin to see the connection between *La Belle Dame Sans Merci* and Shakespeare's sonnet *Like as the Waves*, you will realize that a great poem is the poet's way of illuminating one, or perhaps some, of the facets of the jewel for which all men secretly long—the jewel of Truth.

16. "s" as in "soon".

s

"s"

> **Symbol:** LOWER CASE S
> **Phonemic classification:** lingua-alveolar voiceless fricative
> **IPA usage:** "soon"; "civilian"
> **American English usage:** same as IPA.

"s" is a voiceless consonant. In producing the sound, the tongue tip is raised to the teeth ridge and slightly hollowed. The sound escapes over the hollowed tip.

a. Exercises:

"S" as in soon.

s s s	s s s	s s s	s	
sis sis sis	sis sis sis	sis sis sis	sis	
sas sas sas	sas sas sas	sas sas sas	sas	
sos sos sos	sos sos sos	sos sos sos	sos	
sus sus sus	sus sus sus	sus sus sus	sus	
sessity	sessity	sessity	ses	
sussity	sussity	sussity	sus	etc.

b. Make a list of fifty words containing these sounds and use them in rhymes which will afford you practice in saying the sound, e.g., sixty, sailors, south.

The Meal

Sebastian Seal,
in shimmering silk,
Sat down to a meal
of Sardine Milk.

A Submarine passed,
with a swish and a shwoo—
He saluted the seal—
"How do you do.
Could I sample your meal—
Oh, Mr. Seal?"

On a plain white saucer—
spotlessly clean,
The seal poured milk,
for the submarine:

Who swallowed it down,
with a suck—
suck—
suck—
so very quickly some of it stuck,
stuck very firm,
for almost an hour,
In the submarine's delicate Conning Tower.

Then he sailed away to Sess-sessie-give,
(That's the land where the Sess-sessie people live)
With a pain in his chest,
through drinking the milk,
served by a seal in a shimmering silk!

—D.L.

The problem that "s" presents to the speaker is one of breath control. Unless you have learn to economize the breath, that is, only to let the amount of breath you use for voice, escape from the lungs while you are speaking, as you say "s", it will be accompanied by a sound like a "hissing of innumerable serpents!" Therefore, this sound affords you excellent practice in holding your ribs out, and using the diaphragm and abdominal press during expiration. It all comes back to the problem of breathing.

If you handle this sound skilfully you will find that it, too, can re-echo the sense of a passage. In Shakespeare's sonnet *When to the Sessions of Sweet Silent Thought* there are many sibilants, and these create the "whispering effect" which Shakespeare intended to achieve.

Shelley, in *To Night,* the poem that follows, also uses these sibilants to re-echo the sense of the poem. The "noiseless noise" of silence which we associate with Night is to be heard in the "hushed" effect of the many sibilants in this poem. Remember the atmosphere appropriate to this poem as you speak it.

To Night

Swiftly walk over the Western wave,
Spirit of Night!
Out of the misty eastern cave,
Where, all the long and lone daylight,
Thou wovest dreams of joy and fear
Which make thee terrible and dear,—
Swift be thy flight!

Wrap thy form in a mantle grey
Star inwrought!
Blind with thine hair the eyes of Day,
Kiss her until she be wearied out,

Then wander o'er city, and sea, and land,
Touching all with thine opiate wand—
Come, long-sought!

When I arose and saw the dawn,
I sigh'd for thee;
When light rode high, and the dew was gone,
And noon lay heavy on flower and tree.
And the weary Day turn'd to his rest,
Lingering like an unloved guest,
I sigh'd for thee.

Thy brother Death came, and cried,
"Wouldst thou me?"
Thy sweet child sleep, the filmy-eyed,
Murmur'd like a noontide bee,
Shall I nestle near thy side?"
"Wouldst thou me?"—and I replied,
"No, not thee!"

Death will come when thou art dead,
Soon, too soon—
Sleep will come when thou art fled;
Of neither would I ask the boon
I ask of thee, beloved Night—
Swift be thine approaching flight,
Come soon, soon!

—Percy Bysshe Shelley.

Notice why Shelley longs for Night, not as other people long for it, that they may be laid asleep in body. He definitely says that Death and Sleep are not substitutes for Night, for these, he supposes, are unconscious states. It is because, freed from the pressure of daylight things, his untrammelled imagination can work, "weaving dreams of joy and fear which make thee terrible and dear".

For Shelley, Night brings an intensification of being, a heightened awareness, a more vivid intellectual and emotional response. Can you think of another poet who loved Night, for reasons different from, but not unlike, Shelley's reasons?

"Dear night! this world's defeat:
The stop to busie fools; cares check
and curb;
The day of spirits; my soul's calm retreat
Which none disturbs!

Christ's progress, and his prayer time,
The hours to which high Heaven doth chime."

The poem concludes with the stanza:

"There is in God (some say)
A deep, but dazzling darkness;
As men here
Say it is late and dusky, because
they
See not all clear;
O, for that night! where I in Him
Might live invisible and dim."

For Vaughan, as for Shelley, the physical eye, busy with the objects day discovers, interferes with the world of imagination, where he enjoys an intenser realization of life. Vaughan in the night, which is for him "the day of spirits"—the time when he enjoys "a heightened consciousness of being" which he finds in the deep but dazzling darkness that is God—is seeking "harmony" as Shelley seeks the freedom of the spirit in which alone his imagination can work. It is another form of harmony.

It is interesting to reflect that Shelley wrote:

"Life like a dome of many coloured glass,
Stains the white radiance of Eternity,"

while Vaughan saw Eternity the other night—

"Like a great ring of pure and endless light,
All white as it was bright."

Vaughan and Shelley have many things in common. Perhaps one day you may be tempted to read more of the poetry of these men. In the meantime, look at the way in which Shelley communicates his ideas.

How are Night and Day imagined?

Could you paint a picture of Night from Shelley's description? If you were speaking the poem would you visualize any change in atmosphere between the words spoken by Death and by Sleep, and any difference in the replies made to these offers?

Find the words in which it is clear that Death will never be welcomed, whereas at another time Sleep might be. Throughout the poem, the poet's emotions are as vividly communicated as the thoughts that he expresses.

When you are saying the poem remember that unless you, too, can interpret those feelings vividly you will convey no part of the truth of this poem.

17. "z" as in "zoo."

Z

"z"

Symbol: LOWER-CASE Z
Phonemic classification: lingua-alveolar voiced fricative
IPA usage: "zoo"; "his boxes"; "xylophone"
American English usage: same as IPA.

As in the case of "s" the sound escapes over the slightly hollowed tongue tip in contact with the upper teeth ridge, but "z" is a voiced consonant while "s" is a breath consonant.

a. Exercises:

z z z	z z z	z
ziz ziz ziz	ziz ziz ziz	ziz
zoz zoz zoz	zoz zoz zoz	zoz
zaz zaz zaz	zaz zaz zaz	zaz
zez zez zez	zez zez zez	zez
zeez zeez zeez	zeez zeez zeez	zeez
zize zize zize	zize zize zize	zize
zaahz zaahz zaahz	zaahz zaahz zaahz	zaahz
zoohz zoohz zoohz	zoohz zoohz zoohz	zoohz

b. Practice saying the following words: zoo, zoology, zebra, zulu, zygote, zion, cause, pause, draws.

   Notice that wherever the letter "s" follows in a final position, a voiced consonant, it is articulated as "z", e.g., ladi*es*(z), glov*es*(z), band*s*(z), bib*s*(z); as compared with hat*s*(s), laugh*s*(s), flat*s*(s).

c. Practice the following nonsense rhyme:

Zoe, Zillah, Deborah—
was a Zebra—
It was easy—
To see she was a Zebra,
who was born near the Zambesi!
Her skirt was striped with black,

Whilst upon her stripey back,
(To protect her from the freezie—
Breezes near Zambesi)
She wore a woolley shirt
Zipped neatly to her skirt.

She's quite the smartest Zebra,
Is Zoe, Zillah, Deborah,

She's the smartest quite by far—
from Zululand
to
Zanzibar!
—D.L.

There are nine examples of the sound "z" in the following extract. Find these and distinguish them from the "s" sound of which also there are many examples.

Extract from "Samson Agonistes"

Come, come, no time for lamentation now,
Nor much more cause, Samson hath quit himself
Like Samson, and heroicly hath finished
A life Heroic, on his Enemies
Fully reveng'd, hath left them years of mourning,
And lamentation to the Sons of Caphtor
Through all Philistian bounds. To Israel
Honour hath left, and freedom, let but them
Find courage to lay hold on this occasion,
To himself and Father's house eternal fame;
And which is best and happiest yet, all this
With God not parted from him, as was fear'd,
But favouring and assisting to the end.
Nothing is here for tears, nothing to wail
Or knock the breast, no weakness, no contempt,
Dispraise, or blame, nothing but well and fair,
And what may quiet us in a death so noble.
—John Milton.

This is a very short extract taken from a play by John Milton. You may know the story of Samson and how, though blinded and seemingly defeated by his enemies, the Philistines, who had captured him, he brought ruin and desolation on them. Here, we have expressed the view of the Israelites. What are the values that are upheld in this extract? They are honor, freedom and courage.

Is there anything said, that expresses a deep faith in God? Is the attitude expressed, rebellious or acquiescent? Would you say that the speaker understands the heroic attitude to life? What for him constitutes a hero?

Is it possible to think differently about these things?

I Think Continually of Those

I think continually of those who were truly great
Who from the womb, remembered the soul's history,
Through corridors of light where the hours are suns
Endless and singing. Whose lovely ambition
Was that their lips, still touched with fire,

Should tell of the Spirit clothed from head to foot in song.
And who hoarded from the Spring branches
The desires falling across their bodies like blossoms.

What is precious is never to forget
The essential delight of the blood drawn from ageless springs
Breaking through rocks in worlds before our earth,
Never to deny its pleasure in the morning simple light,
Nor its grave evening demand for love.
Never to allow gradually the traffic to smother,
With noise and fog the flowering of the Spirit.

Near the snow, near the sun, in the highest fields,
See how these names are fêted by the waving grass
And by streamers of white cloud
And whispers of wind in the listening sky.
The names of those who in their lives fought for life,
Who wore at their hearts the fire's centre,
Born of the sun they travelled a short while towards the sun,
And left the vivid air signed with their honour.

—Stephen Spender

This poem express a quite different idea of what is truly heroic. The extract from *Samson Agonistes* is in praise of doing. The hero is a man of action. But Stephen Spender's poem is in praise of being, of "those who in their lives fought for life". These, it is claimed, are truly brave. How can anyone in his life fight for life?

Do you think Elizabeth Fry when she fought for improvement in the conditions of people in prisons was fighting "for life"? Read through the following list of "activities" and say which of them represents, in your opinion, a good way of "fighting for life".

1. To try to discover a cure for cancer.
2. To make a slum.
3. To try to discover a cure for the common cold.
4. To gormandise.
5. To write a Bach Prelude.
6. To make an atomic bomb.
7. To make a botanical garden or park.
8. To kill a lion.
9. To build and endow a theatre where the great plays of the world can be produced.
10. To overwork a donkey.
11. To build a day care center.
12. To hoard up gold.
13. To write "Hamlet".

14. To burn people who do not believe what you believe.
15. To be jealous of those who succeed.
16. To save someone from drowning.
17. To carry out experiments in the improvement of crops.
18. To paint Leonardo da Vinci's picture of the "Last Supper".
19. To enjoy a day in Spring.
20. To set up a factory for making good rubber tyres.

You will notice that some are concerned with physical life, and some are concerned with the life of the mind, or of the spirit. Classify them under these headings, leaving out whichever activities, in your opinion, destroy rather than promote life. In every case give your reason for the opinion you hold.

It is a simple thing to understand what can be done to fight for life compared with the more difficult thing that Stephen Spender tells us about in his poem. He claims that the truly great are not what the world calls heroes, but the people who love and value and enjoy being alive in their five senses. They are the people who understand the art of living. Their love of life is symbolized in the fact that they remember that the sun is the source of all life, and the song on their lips symbolizes their joy in life. The important thing, perhaps, is that we are reminded that the spirit of man is fed through the responses of his senses.

Many great thinkers have reminded us of it. Wordsworth knew it, though he expressed it differently. So did the man who wrote "release my soul through every door of sense"; and Raleigh sums it up in the verse:

Not in vain he lives,
Who has known,
A single May day.

People who are not "truly great" in the way Stephen Spender means are "animated corpses" who have eyes and they see not; ears and they hear not.

Now read the poem below and then say whether it has anything to say on the subject of heroism. Here you will find yet another attitude to this subject:

An Irish Airman Foresees His Death

I know that I shall meet my fate
Somewhere among the clouds above;
Those that I fight I do not hate,
Those that I guard I do not love;

My country is Kiltartan Cross,
My countrymen Kiltartan's poor,
No likely end could bring them loss
Or leave them happier than before.

Nor law, nor beauty bade me fight,
Nor public men, nor cheering crowds,
A lonely impulse of delight
Drove to this tumult in the clouds;

I balanced all, brought all to mind,
The years to come seemed waste of breath,
A waste of breath the years behind
In balance with this life, this death.
—*W. B. Yeats.*

There have been times in the past when men have been happy to "die for their country". In doing so they have been considered heroes who in battle protected their countrymen at the expense of their lives. They were, and still are, called patriots.

This particular airman says he is not one of them. He knows that it is very likely that he will die in battle, but his reason for being in the battle is not love of his own people, or hatred of their enemies:

"Those that I fight I do not hate,
Those that I guard I do not love"

Why is he there, then? It is because he enjoys the heightened consciousness of being alive which he experiences in a situation, where all his skill, and know ledge, and experience are pitted against the dangerous and incalculable elements of Nature.

This is an adventurous man. An aeroplane is to him what a ship was to Columbus. The sky is to him what the sea was to Columbus, a challenge—a victory—a defeat? He does not know. But it is his own response to the challenge that he enjoys. Why, then, does he not buy an aeroplane, or make it, and fly it?

The answer is in the poem:

My country is Kiltartan Cross,
My countrymen Kiltartan's poor,
No likely end could bring them loss
Or leave them happier than before.

He is a poor man born and brought up in an Irish village, surrounded by people who lead circumscribed lives, with little ability, or opportunity, or vision, or ambition. His prospect is a bleak one of monotonous routine in the effort to earn his daily bread. He would never be able to afford so expensive a thing as an aeroplane.

But in war, aeroplanes are not luxuries, they are necessities, and the poorest man, provided he will risk his life, and has the skill, may fly one.

This man flies his aircraft not because he wants to kill anyone, but because only by joining up as an airman can he enjoy the exercise of his skill as a pilot, and he makes his choice deliberately. He is obviously the kind of man who would choose "one crowded hour of glorious life" rather than an age of "partly living", which seems to be his prospect otherwise, in a mechanical and monotonous civilization where everyone is so bent on the achievement of material security that life has been robbed of all sense of adventure.

Here is a man who does not want to be safe. He wants to feel and to know that he is alive, and one can only do that when one is pitting all one's powers—physical, mental and spiritual—against the problems of an accepted challenge.

Do you think he was a hero or a villain?

Do you think he was more civilized or less civilized since he did not love people merely because they were born in the same village, or town, or country? Do you get the impression that he liked humanity?

Do you think he believed in war?

Do you think all is well with a society in which only in war can men feel again the joy of adventure?

Do you agree that it is better to live dangerously or to live timorously?

It is a very stimulating and interesting poem, for it makes us think about things that are important to us as human beings.

18. "sh" as in "short".

ʃ

"SH"

Symbol: ESH

Phonemic classification: linqua-palatal voiceless fricative

IPA usage: "short"; "surely"; "ocean"

American English usage: same as IPA.

In shaping this sound the hollow space made by the tongue which has been raised to the teeth ridge, is much broader than in the case of "s" or "z". Through this aperture the sound escapes. [ʃ] is a voiceless consonant.

a. Exercises:

sh sh sh	sh sh sh	sh
shish shish shish	shish shish shish	shish
shosh shosh shosh	shosh shosh shosh	shosh
shush shush shush	shush shush shush	shush
sheesh sheesh sheesh	sheesh sheesh sheesh	sheesh
shoshity	shoshity	shosh
shushity	shushity	shush
shashity	shashity	shash etc.

b. Make a list of words containing this sound, e.g., shine, shiver, shock.

c. Make up nonsense rhymes which will give you practice in saying this sound.

d. Say the following poem aloud until you know it by heart:

The Sea and the Skylark

On ear and ear two noises too old to end
Trench—right, the tide that ramps against the shore,
With a flood or a fall, low lull-off or all roar,
Frequenting there while moon shall wear and wend.

Left hand, off land, I hear the lark ascend,
His rash-fresh re-winded new-skeined score
In crisps of curl off wild winch whirl, and pour
And pelt music, till none's to spill nor spend.

How these two shame this shallow and frail town:
How ring right out our sordid turbid time,
Being pure: We, life's pride and cared-for crown,

Have lost that cheer and charm of earth's past prime:
Our make and making break, are breaking, down
To man's last-dust, drain fast towards man's first slime.
—Gerard Manley Hopkins.

What is the poem about?

Is there any evidence that the author of this poem is as sensitive to impressions of sound as of sight?

In his description, he is intent on communicating these sounds to us in such a way that we shall not only hear them, but respond as he does to this expression of tireless and unending vitality.

He makes us notice the quality of, and the variations in, the sound of the sea. Its strength and power is expressed in the words "ramp" and "roar", which brings to mind the behavior of a lion. The music of the sea is heard in the words "with a flood or a fall, low lull-off". It is not an accident that the poet uses so many clear and dark "l" sounds to communicate the quiet contrast of the ebb with the noisy rolled "r's" of "ramp" and "roar", which describe the flow of the tide.

Notice how many words expressing action are used in the fourth line of this poem. Why is "frequenting" a perfect choice? What effect is achieved by the repetition of the "w" sound?

In the second stanza, notice the use of plosives to communicate the impression of a tireless and ungrudging expenditure of energy, and the sense of joyous excitement created in us by the words "pour and pelt", "spill nor spend". They express a generous outpouring of wealth from an inexhaustible source. That is the impression.

Notice the use of the voiced plosives in "break, breaking down", where the energy being used is forced and hard, giving a sense of conflict and resistance as compared with the lightness and ease of activity expressed in the aspirated "p" of pour, pelt, spill and spend.

The Sea and the Skylark are here used by the poet as symbols of Nature as opposed to the shallow and frail town which is a symbol of industrial civilization—something highly artificial.

The poet, by contrasting the state of man with the state of the sea and the skylark, reminds us that man is an animal who belongs to Nature, just as much as do the sea and the skylark, but he is false to his being, whereas they are true to theirs. Find the words that express the idea that he is false. First, we are told that the sea and the skylark are "pure". Then the poet goes on to use words like shallow, frail, sordid, turbid in his description of the artificial world man has created. Finally we are reminded that the soul and spirit of man was not nurtured in that environment. He evolved in obedience to the same laws of life as those which control the sea and the skylark. His present situation, false and unnatural as it is, though created by himself, will reduce him ultimately to the lowest and most degraded form of life. Find the lines in which this view is expressed. Is there any evidence in this poem that the writer lived at a time when men had heard of biological evolution?

Go back and read this poem with the vitality, the intelligence, the imagination, the sensitiveness and the technical control needed to convey the truth as this poet has expressed it.

19. "zh" as in "pleasure"

ʒ

"ZH"

Symbol: YOGH
Phonemic classification: lingua-palatal voiced fricative
IPA usage: "pleasure"; "visionary"; beige"
American English usage: same as IPA.

The [Z] sound is shaded exactly the same way as the [S] sound, the difference being that [Z] is a voiced consonant.

a. Exercises:

zhizh zhizh zhizh　　zhizh zhizh zhizh　　zhizh
zhozh zhozh zhozh　　zhozh zhozh zhozh　　zhozh
zhuzh zhuzh zhuzh　　zhuzh zhuzh zhuzh　　zhuzh
zhoozh zhoozh zhoozh　　zhoozh zhoozh zhoozh　　zhoozh
zhizhity　　zhizhity　　zhizhity　　zhizhity　　zhizhity
zhozhity　　zhozhity　　zhozhity　　zhozhity　　zhozhity
zhuzhity　　zhuzhity　　zhuzhity　　zhuzhity　　zhuzhity

b. Make a list of fifty words containing this sound and say these words, e.g., measure, leisure, pleasure, azure.
c. Make up a nonsense rhyme which will give you further practice, e.g.:

Zhing Zhang Zh-Zhoomy Zhunkle
Was the name of Penelope's Uncle,
Penelope's Uncle, who
in his leisure,

Looked and looked all day for treasure—
Buried treasure, beneath a tin,
With a large, round rolling pin,
And a sixpenny tea-cup measure,
In which he could deposit the treasure.

He found a spider beneath the tin,
An azure beetle, very thin
But though he looked,
and scratched and scraped,
The buried treasure always escaped.
AND
Now he's called
Zhing Zhang Zh-Zhoomy,
Penelope's Uncle,
always gloomy.

—D.L.

The next poem, *Kubla Khan*, is given to you not merely for practice in saying the sound "ZH", but because it affords excellent practice in perfecting and finishing both vowel and consonant sounds and in gaining control of your power to use pause, pace, emphasis, and an unfaltering rhythmic sense to convey both the pictures and feelings expressed in this fragment of poetry, which one can never read without a feeling of regret that Coleridge did not complete so enchanting and exquisite a poetic experience. Try to explain the reasons for the "enchantment" of this poem. Can you find in it elements that are:

a. Exotic?
b. Strange?
c. Remote?
d. Terrifying?
e. Supernatural?

Choose a picture which you think could properly be described as "exquisite". Choose a sentence or sentences in which the sound re-echoes the sense. Explain briefly what the effect is and how it is achieved.

Do you notice any changes in the movement of the poem? How are these effects obtained?

If you were trying to describe the difference in the atmosphere created by the description of the chasm and the description of the damsel with a dulcimer, which words would you use from the following list:

terrifying	serene	eerie	strange
haunting	enchanted	tranquil	gloomy
weird	exotic	savage	mysterious

Kubla Khan

In Xanadu did Kubla Khan
A stately pleasure-dome decree:
Where Alph, the sacred river, ran
Through caverns measureless to man
   Down to a sunless sea.
So twice five miles of fertile ground
With walls and towers were girdled round:
And there were gardens bright with sinuous rills
Where blossom'd many an incense-bearing tree;
And here were forests ancient as the hills
Enfolding sunny spots of greenery.

But O, that deep romantic chasm which slanted
Down the green hill athwart a cedarn cover!
A savage place! as holy and enchanted
As e'er beneath a waning moon was haunted
By woman wailing for her demon-lover!
And from this chasm, with ceaseless turmoil seething,
As if this earth in fast thick pants were breathing,
A mighty fountain momently was forced;
Amid whose swift half-intermitted burst
Huge fragments vaulted like rebounding hail,
Or chaffy grain beneath the thresher's flail:
And 'mid these dancing rocks at once and ever
It flung up momently the sacred river.
Five miles meandering with a mazy motion
Through wood and dale the sacred river ran,
Then reach'd the caverns measureless to man,
And sank in tumult to a lifeless ocean;
And 'mid this tumult Kubla heard from far
Ancestral voices prophesying war!
   The shadow of the dome of pleasure
   Floated midway on the waves;
Where was heard the mingled measure
   From the fountain and the caves.
It was a miracle of rare device,
A sunny pleasure dome with caves of ice!

A damsel with a dulcimer
In a vision once I saw:
It was an Abyssinian maid,

And on her dulcimer she played,
Singing of Mount Abora.
Could I revive within me,
Her symphony and song,
To such a deep delight 'twould win me,
That with music loud and long,
I would build that dome in air,
That sunny dome! those caves of ice!
And all who heard should see them there,
And all should cry, Beware! Beware!
His flashing eyes, his floating hair!
Weave a circle round him thrice,
And close your eyes with holy dread,
For he on honey-dew hath fed,
And drunk the milk of Paradise.

—*S.T. Coleridge.*

20. "ch" as in "church".

tʃ

"CH"

Symbol: LOWER-CASE T/ESH
Phonemic classification: lingua-palatal voiceless affricative
IPA usage: "church"; "thatch"
American English usage: same as IPA.

"ch" is a breath consonant. In producing the sound, the tongue tip is in the same position as it is in shaping [t] or [d], and the fact that these are not the sounds produced is due to the slow release of the tongue tip from its contact with the teeth ridge.

If the contact is released quickly, the sound produced is [t] or [d]; if it is done slowly, the sound produced is quite different. It is, in fact, [ch] or [j], as the case may be.

In phonetics "ch" has the symbol [tʃ]; "j" has the symbol [dʒ]. I wonder who first found out that the slow release of the contact of the tongue tip with the teeth ridge produced quite a different sound from that made by releasing the contact quickly.

That is one of the fascinating things about speech studies. They can lead you back to the beginning of things, for in speech is mirrored the whole adventure of living. It is called into being by man's developing awareness of his world, and if your world is narrow, and intellectually and emotionally impoverished, so also will your speech be. In the end it is the measure of *you*!

a. Exercises:

ch ch ch	ch ch ch	ch
church church church	church church church	church
choch choch choch	choch choch choch	choch
chich chich chich	chich chich chich	chich
chawch chawch chawch	chawch chawch chawch	chawch
chichity	chichity	chichity
chochety	chochety	chochety
churchity	churchity	churchity etc.

b. Make a list of fifty words containing this sound. Use these words in rhymes which will afford you practice in saying the sound, e.g., church, chopper, Chippendale, chicken, chop, Chesterfield, chutney, chisel.

c. Practice the following rhyme:

Said the Chop to the Chopper,
"Sir—
I do not think it proper,
sir,
The way you chop at random,
Nearly everyone you meet.
Those chrysanthemums,
and cherries,
And the Chesterfield suite—
Then the Chippendale chair,
The way you chopped it, wasn't fair."

Said the Chop,
"It's plain to me,
That what you lack is chivalry!"

A Cheetah,
and cheese,
And charming summer breeze—
All shouted in a chorus,
"Oh chop—oh chop, beware,
Let the chopper, chop and chop
The Chippendale chair—
Let him chop chrysanthemums—
Chesterfields too—
But never ever criticise, in case,
The chopper chops, at you!"

—D.L.

d. Practice the following poem:

Tarantella

Do you remember an Inn,
Miranda?
Do you remember an Inn,
And the tedding and the spreading
Of the straw for a bedding,
And the fleas that tease in the high Pyrenees,
And the wine that tasted of the tar?

And the cheers and the jeers of the young muleteers,
(Under the dark of the vine verandah?)
Do you remember an Inn, Miranda,
Do you remember an Inn?

And the cheers and the jeers of the young muleteers,
Who! hadn't got a penny,
And who weren't paying any,
And the hammer at the doors and the din?

And the Hip! Hop! Hap!
Of the clap
Of the hands to the twirl and the swirl
Of the girl gone chancing,
Glancing,
Dancing,
Backing and advancing,
Snapping of the clapper to the spin
Out and in—
And the ting, tong, tang of the guitar!
Do you remember an Inn,
Miranda?
Do you remember an Inn?

Never more;
Miranda,
Never more.
Only the high peaks hoar:
And Aragon a torrent at the door.
No sound
In the walls of the halls where falls
The tread

Of the feet of the dead to the ground.
No sound:
Only the boom
Of the far waterfall like Doom.
—*Hilaire Belloc.*

Pace is tremendously important in this poem, which has great variety of pace and will therefore give you plenty of practice as a speaker in the management of pace, as well as in the power to communicate a change of mood and atmosphere.

To say this poem well, on the technical side you require a very flexible and agile tongue tip, but though the poem moves at a quicker and a quicker pace, mounting to a climax as does the movement of the dance, which is the basis of the rhythm of this poem, you must not make the mistake of trying to get the climax merely by the speed at which you say the words. You will succeed in your interpretation better if you convey an impression of speed through the use of intensity which is a matter of volume and breath control. Remember to finish off final consonants!

Try to convey the mood of gaiety and joyful abandon that so captured the imagination of the poet. How would you describe the change of atmosphere expressed in the last stanza? What has happened to the inn? What means has the poet used to create a sense of doom? In speaking this poem would there be any perceptible change in the pace of the last stanza?

Can you think of any other poem which is the expression of a mood?

21. "j" as in "judge".

dʒ

SOFT "G"
OR "J"

Symbol: Lower case D/YOGH
Phonemic classification: lingua-palatal voiced affricative
IPA usage: "judg*e*" ; "George"
American English usage: same as IPA.

This is a voiced consonant. It is produced by the slow release of the plosive [d]. It is, therefore, a consonant shaped by the tongue tip slowly released from contact with the ridge behind the upper teeth.

a. Exercises:

j j j	j j j	j j j	j
jej jej jej	jej jej jej	jej jej jej	jej
jij jij jij	jij jij jij	jij jij jij	jij
joj joj joj	joj joj joj	joj joj joj	joj
juj juj juj	juj juj juj	juj juj juj	juj
jeej jeej jeej	jeej jeej jeej	jeej jeej jeej	jeej
johj johj johj	johj johj johj	johj johj johj	johj
jooj jooj jooj	jooj jooj jooj	jooj jooj jooj	jooj

b. Make a list of fifty words containing this sound and say the e.g., judge, Jerusalem, Jericho, jelly, jam, George.
c. Distinguish carefully between the initial sounds in the following words: jewel, duel: jew, dew: juke, duke: juice, deuce.
d. Here is perhaps the most famous nonsense rhyme in the world, and certainly the one which, above all others, you should know by heart:

Jabberwocky

'Twas brillig, and the slithy toves
Did gyre and gimble in the wabe;
All mimsy were the borogoves,
And the mome raths outgrabe.

Beware the Jabberwock, my son!
The jaws that bite, the claws that catch!
Beware the Jubjub Bird and shun
The frumious Bandersnatch!

He took his vorpal sword in hand:
Long time the manxome foe he sought—
So rested he by the Tum-Tum tree,
And stood awhile in thought.

And as in uffish thought he stood,
The Jabberwock, with eyes of flame,
Came whiffling through the tulgey wood
And burbled as it came!

One, two! One, two! and through and through
The vorpal blade went snicker-snack!
He left it dead and with its head
He went galumphing back.

"And hast thou slain the Jabberwock?
Come to my arms, my beamish boy!
O frabjous day! Callooh! Callay!"
He chortled in his joy.

'Twas brillig, and the slithy toves
Did gyre and gimble in the wabe;
All mimsy were the borogoves,
And the mome raths outgrabe.

—Lewis Carroll.

What do you suppose *Jabberwocky* is about?

Of what does the Jabberwock remind you?

Try to find out the normal word or words a suggestion of which lies behind each of the "invented" words in the poem. Do you believe that the man who wrote this poem believed that sound should re-echo sense? Where do you find him most successful in achieving this?

Do you think that Lewis Carroll has any sense of humour? If you do, quote two instances of it from the poem. Do you enjoy this poem or do you think it merely silly?

What do you notice about the metre of each stanza? Does the poet achieve anything by making the last line shorter than the preceding lines in each stanza.

How would you describe the movement of these stanzas? Is the movement suitable to the subject of the poem? In what way? Do you think this is an accident or do you think the poem shows a mastery of the physical and intellectual aspects of language?

Is there any evidence in this poem that Lewis Carroll had an original mind?

e. Practice the following Psalm:

Psalm 137

By the rivers of Babylon, there we sat down, yea, we wept
when we remembered Zion.
We hanged our harps upon the willows in the midst thereof.
For there they that carried us away captive required of us
a song; and they that wasted us required of us mirth, saying:
Sing us one of the songs of Zion.
How shall we sing the Lord's song in a strange land?
If I forget thee, O Jerusalem, let my right hand forget her
cunning.
If I do not remember thee, let my tongue cleave to the roof
of my mouth; if I prefer not Jerusalem above my chief joy.
Remember, O Lord the children of Edom in the day of
Jerusalem; who said: Raze it, raze it, even to the foundation
thereof.
O daughter of Babylon, who art to be destroyed; happy
shall he be, that rewardeth thee as thou hast served us.

You will notice that it has been chosen because it affords some practice in the use of the "j" sound, but at the same time it presents a complete contrast to *Jabberwocky* from every point of view. The one is an expression of triumph and pride in achievement, the other is an expression of defeat and desire for revenge.

Why did they "hang their harps on willows"? With what state of feeling do these captives associate the impulse to sing?

Of what is Jerusalem the symbol in this poet's mind? Can you find in this poem any expression of the emotion of hate? Is there any evidence in this poem that the author believed in the existence of God? Can you find any evidence that the faith expressed is unconquerable?

Now that you have thought about the situation and the feelings expressed in this Psalm, and realized that they are normal, human thoughts, and feelings, evoked by being defeated in battle, will you refrain from speaking the words of the Bible in a monotonous, parsonical voice? Be certain that what you say means something, and say it as though it did, giving full value to the ideas, and to the feelings that accompany these ideas.

There is no better book for the student of speech than the Bible.

It is full of wonderful and enthralling stories of adventure and experience. These are well expressed, and so afford the speaker rich material on which to train his voice. But first of all he must get out of the habit of intoning passages from the Bible in a monotonous chant.

The Bible is a record of human experience. It is "memorable speech," and as a speaker your task is to bring out fully the thoughts and feelings it expresses. You cannot do this if you let your brain sleep while your voice continues to operate.

22. "y" as in "yet."

j

"y"

Symbol: LOWER-CASE J
Phonemic classification: lingua-palatal glide (semi-vowel).
IPA usage: "yet", "union"
American English usage: same as IPA.

This is a palatal sound, made by the blade of the tongue recoiling from a partial contact with the mid-palate.

Like "h" and "w", the sound "y" is classed as a semi-vowel, and practice in saying this sound has already been given.

a. Exercises:

yip yip yip	yip yip yip	yip yip yip	yip
yap yap yap	yap yap yap	yap yap yap	yap
yep yep yep	yep yep yep	yep yep yep	yep
yop yop yop	yop yop yop	yop yop yop	yop
yup yup yup	yup yup yup	yup yup yup	yup
yippy yippy yippy	yippy yippy yippy	yippy yippy yippy	
yappy yappy yappy	yappy yappy yappy	yappy yappy yappy	
yuppy yuppy yuppy	yuppy yuppy yuppy	yuppy yuppy yuppy	
yoppy yoppy yoppy	yoppy yoppy yoppy	yoppy yoppy yoppy	

b. Make a list of words containing this sound and say the words aloud, e.g., yet, yellow, you, year.

c. Practice the following nonsense rhyme:

A yellow canary
yawned on a yew,
Then
sang to yak,
with a yacht on his back—
"How do you do, Mr. Yak
Why have you tied that yacht on your back,
Mr. Yak,
Mr. Yak?"

"I've just had a feast,
on some yeast"
Said the Yak.
"Very soon I will float,
like a boat,
And this yacht on my back,
Will guide me all through—
Countries a-new."

"New-York, Yokohama,
I'll buy a yash-mak—
That's why I've got the yacht on my back,"
said the Yak!

—D.L.

d. Say aloud the following verses:

O Dreamy, Gloomy, Friendly Trees!

O dreamy, gloomy, friendly Trees,
I came along your narrow track
To bring my gifts unto your knees
And gifts did you give back;
For when I brought this heart that burns—
These thoughts that bitterly repine—
And laid them here among the ferns
and the hum of boughs divine,
Ye vastest breathers of the air,
Shook down with slow and mighty poise
Your coolness on the human care,
Your wonder on its toys,
Your greenness on the heart's despair,
Your darkness on its noise.

—Herbert Trench.

Notice in the above poem that "y" in the first line represents the short "i" [ɪ] sound, and avoid saying it as long "ee".

Does the speaker think that trees have any effect on him? What is the effect? Would you say that the person speaking was a happy person? Give reasons for your answer. For what characteristics does he appreciate these trees? This is not an easy poem to speak well. It needs to be quietly spoken, but not monotonously. It is a poem in which the pace is slow, but that does not mean it should lack variety. Look at the following lines:

Shook down with slow and mighty poise
Your coolness on the human care,

"With slow and mighty poise" should be said at a quicker pace and in a lower key than "Shook down . . . your coolness on the human care", which is the main idea of this sentence, and must be kept clear, in spite of the interruption that the phrase "with slow and mighty poise" represents.

When a phrase or clause interrupts, as it were, the main meaning of the sentence, though it adds something to the meaning, the speaker should pause before and after such a phrase, or clause, and speak it at a quicker pace and at a lower pitch than he uses before and after such a phrase or clause, which is known as a parenthesis.

"And we'll rise,/you'll rise as I rise,/
Not because we would, but because we must."

"You'll rise as I rise" is a clause in parenthesis. Speak it at a quicker pace and on a lower pitch than the rest of the sentence.

Make a collection of examples of parenthesis and practice saying these until you acquire skill in speaking a passage that contains a parenthesis.

23. "k" as in "king".

k

"k"

Symbols: LOWER-CASE K
Phonemic classification: lingua-velar voiceless stop-plosive
IPA usage: "king"; "back"
American English usage: same as IPA.

This is known as a velar consonant. There are three such consonants: "k", "g" and "ng".

The sound follows the release of the contact of the base of the tongue with the soft palate.

a. Exercises:

k k k	k k k	k k k	k
kik kik kik	kik kik kik	kik kik kik	kik

kek kek kek	kek kek kek	kek kek kek	kek
kak kak kak	kak kak kak	kak kak kak	kak
kok kok kok	kok kok kok	kok kok kok	kok
kuk kuk kuk	kuk kuk kuk	kuk kuk kuk	kuk
kickity	kickity	kickity	kick
kockity	kockity	kockity	kock
kukety	kukety	kukety	kuk
kakety	kakety	kakety	kak
kookety	kookety	kookety	kook
keekety	kawkety	keekety	keek
kawkety	kohkety	kawkety	kawk
kohkety	keekety	kohkety	kohk

b. Make up a list of fifty words containing this sound, e.g., kangaroo, cause, capable, convince, khaki, kind, kid, kettle, kindle, koala, cambric, king, cure, kilt, quaint, quick, quake, queen, quest.

c. Make up nonsense rhymes to give you practice in saying this sound, e.g.:

In the Zoo,
at Kalamazoo,
Lived the quaintest Kangaroo,
Who capered around in kilt of khaki,
calling loudly—
"Quick, look at me,
quite the cleverest Kangaroo,
ever to live in Kalamazoo."

From a eucalyptus tree,
Koala Bear called,
"You look at me,
Eating leaves, and then, I'm told,
My breath will cure the common cold,
I'm the King of Kalamazoo,
cleverer far than the Kangaroo."

A tiny chicken, in Kalamazoo,
heard this talk of these animals two,
"I wouldn't," it cheeriped, "be quite so bold,
to say I could cure the common cold.
I can't even wear a kilt of khaki,
and yet I'm convinced that it's really me,
who's cleverer far than both of you,
the reason, of course, I don't live in a Zoo!"
—D.L.

d. The following extract from *As You Like It* will not only give you practice in saying "k" sounds. It may serve to kindle your interest in the play from which the extract is taken:

Selection from "As You Like It", Act III scene ii

Rosalind: *There is a man haunts the forest that abuses our young plants with carving Rosalind on their barks; hangs odes upon hawthorns, and elegies on brambles; all, forsooth, deifying the name of Rosalind: if I could meet that fancymonger I would give him some good counsel, for he seems to have the quotidian of love upon him.*

Orlando: *I am he that is so love-shaked: I pray you, tell me your remedy.*

Rosalind: *There is none of my uncle's marks upon you: he taught me how to know a man in love; in which cage of rushes I am sure you are not a prisoner.*

Orlando: *What were his marks?*

Rosalind: *A lean cheek; which you have not: a blue eye and sunken; which you have not: an unquestionable spirit; which you have not: a beard neglected; which you have not: but I pardon you for that; for simply your having in beard is a younger brother's revenue: Then your hose should be ungartered, your bonnet unbanded, your sleeve unbuttoned, your shoe untied, and everything about you demonstrating a careless desolation. But you are no such man; you are rather point-device in your accoutrements; as loving yourself than seeming the lover of any other.*

—*William Shakespeare.*

Could you tell from this extract that Rosalind is a tease?

Has she a lively mind?

Is she witty?

You cannot hope to say this extract well unless you are prepared to find out more about the characters of Rosalind and Orlando. To do this you must read the whole play. It is worth reading, because it is a very well written play. What are the tests of a good play? One test is the author's power of creating character. Shakespeare had this power to an astonishing degree.

Have you ever thought how you come by the impressions you have of the characters of people? Let us try to think it out.

We know them by:

1. What they say.
2. The manner in which they say it.
3. What other people say to them.
4. How they say it.

5. What they say about them.
6. What they do.
7. What other people do to them.

When you have read the whole of *As You Like It* you will find that you have made the acquaintance of a great many interesting and well-contrasted characters.

How does the banished Duke differ from the usurping Duke? Be sure that whatever you say about him you can prove from the text of the play. How does Jacques differ from Touchstone? Describe the three sons of Sir Rowland de Bois, Oliver, Orlando, and Jacques. How do Celia and Rosalind differ from each other?

Shakespeare was the great geographer of human nature. To read his plays is to increase our knowledge and understanding of human beings.

Do you want to know and understand human beings? If so, why do you? No two people speak exactly alike, yet they speak like themselves. So when you are saying this extract you should try to convey in the tones of your voice the fact that first Rosalind speaks and then she is answered by Orlando. How can you do this? You might do it by making Orlando speak at a slower pace, on a slightly lower pitch and with greater resonance than you use for Rosalind. Also you might indicate a change in position for Rosalind and Orlando, by changing the direction of your eyes. But whatever you do, don't move your feet about. Stand still, and remember you are speaking to someone. Do not recite. Visualize Rosalind and Orlando all the time and try to make their speech sound as natural as possible.

Below is a most entertaining extract in which the sound echoes the sense.

The Frogs (Aristophanes)

O brood of the mere and the spring,
Gather together and sing
From the depths of your throat,
By the side of the boat
Co-ax as we move in a ring:
Co-ax, co-ax, co-ax,
Brekekekex, co-ax.

Dionysus:
Don't sing any more;
I begin to be sore!

Frogs:
Brekekekex co-ax.
Co-ax, co-ax, co-ax,
Brekekekex co-ax!

Dionysus:
Is it nothing to you
If I'm black and I'm blue?

Frogs:
Brekekekex co-ax!

Dionysus:
A plague on all of your swarming packs,
There's nothing in you except co-ax!

Frogs:
Co-ax, co-ax, co-ax,
Brekekekex co-ax.

Dionysus:
Peace musical sisters,
I'm covered with blisters.

Frogs:
Brekekekex, co-ax,
Co-ax, co-ax, co-ax,
Brekekekex, co-ax.
Our song we can double,
Without the least trouble,
Brekekekex, co-ax.

—*Extract from Gilbert Murray's Translation.*

Did you not find a great deal of amusement in imitating the noise of frogs?

You will find a great number of exercises have been given for "k". This is because many people suffer from a flabby, soft palate, which makes speech woolly and tends to encourage nasalization of consonants, for when the soft palate drops, some of the voice, which should come through the oral cavity, escapes through the nostrils and speech then has a nasal twang. These exercises are as much exercises for toning up the soft palate as for improving the [k] sound.

24. "g" as in "glory".

g

HARD "G"

Symbol: LOWER-CASE G
Phonemic classification: lingua-velar voiced stop-plosive
IPA usage: "glory"; "beggar"
American English usage: same as IPA.

This is a voiced consonant. The sound follows the release of the contact of the base of the tongue with the soft palate. Practice this sound as it is good exercise for the soft palate and will help to eliminate any tendency to nasal twang.

a. Exercises:

g g g	g g g	g g g	g
gig gig gig	gig gig gig	gig gig gig	gig
geg geg geg	geg geg geg	geg geg geg	geg
gag gag gag	gag gag gag	gag gag gag	gag
gog gog gog	gog gog gog	gog gog gog	gog
gug gug gug	gug gug gug	gug gug gug	gug
guggity	guggity	guggity	gug
goggity	goggity	goggity	gog
googity	googity	googity	goog
geggity	geggity	geggity	geg

b. Make a list of fifty words which have this sound. Do not confuse this sound with the [dʒ] as in ja̲m, e.g., goose—juice, gum—gem, give—jive.

c. Use these words in nonsense rhymes which will give you further practice:

I glimpsed a green geranium
garbed in gaberdine,
Gorgeous gems
were round the hems,
Of each petal—in between—
each leaf,
a sheaf,
of garlic—
Tied in place with grey georgette—
Gentle whisps of grey georgette.

So there it grew, the green geranium,
such a happy green geranium,
With gesticulating leaves,
speaking French to foreign breeze,
Dancing stem a-whirl,
Like a gracious geisha-girl!

—D.L.

c. Say aloud the following extract from Act II, scene iii of *Macbeth:*

The Murder of Duncan

Macbeth.—*Go bid thy mistress, when my drink is ready,*
She strike upon the bell. Get thee to bed.—[Exit Servant.
Is this a dagger which I see before me,
The handle toward my hand? Come, let me clutch thee.
I have thee not, and yet I see thee still.
Art thou not, fatal vision, sensible

To feeling as to sight? or art thou but
A dagger of the mind, a false creation,
Proceeding from the heat-oppressed brain?
I see thee yet, in form as palpable
As this which now I draw,
Thou marshall'st me the way that I was going
And such an instrument I was to use.
Mine eyes are made the fools o' the other senses,
Or else worth all the rest; I see thee still,
And on thy blade and dudgeon gouts of blood,
Which was not so before.—There's no such thing:
It is the bloody business which informs
Thus to mine eyes. Now o'er the one-half-world
Nature seems dead, and wicked dreams abuse
The curtain'd sleep; witchcraft celebrates
Pale Hecate's offerings; and wither'd murder,
Alarm'd by his sentinel the wolf,
Whose howl's his watch, thus with his stealthy pace,
Moves like a ghost.—Thou sure and firm-set earth,
Hear not my steps, which way they walk, for fear
Thy very stones prate of my whereabouts,
And take the present horror from the time,
Which now suits with it.—Whiles I threat, he lives:
Words to the heat of deeds too cold breath gives.
[A bell rings.
I go, and it is done; the bell invites me.
Hear it not, Duncan, for it is a knell
That summons thee to heaven or to hell. [Exit.

—*William Shakespeare.*

It would be a fine thing if, after reading this passage from *Macbeth*, you felt, if you had never read the play before, that now you want to go at once and read it. Read it aloud, learning to say the words in character, to speak as Macbeth would speak, which is not the same way as Banquo or Lady Macbeth, or the Three Witches, for every human being speaks like himself. The state of his physical being, the pace at which his mind works, the liveliness of his imagination are all reflected in the way in which he says things.

Macbeth has a very lively imagination. Much more lively than the imagination of most people, but the interesting thing about it is that it only works when he is under great nervous and emotional stress. The really civilized person is one whose imagination is at work at all times, so that he can look before and after and see the truth about every situation.

Macbeth is about to murder Duncan as you can realize from this extract. All his senses are alert and even "on edge".

What are the ideas and images that Shakespeare uses to make us feel the terror and the strain in the mind of Macbeth?

> The ghostly dagger.
> Wicked dreams.
> The howl of the wolf.
> Witchcraft.
> Moves like a ghost.
> Thy very stones prate of my whereabouts.

They are images of fear and darkness—Silence, startled only by the terrifying howl of the wolf, the horror of the death he intends, driven home by the idea of even the dead stones coming to life to denounce him. You cannot speak this passage in a calm voice at an even and monotonous pace. You must live every emotion that Macbeth experiences and express it in your voice. But be careful; do not merely "indulge" in feeling, and dramatize the situation by "dripping feeling" over every word. There are infinite gradations of feeling, as the horror reaches its climax, and unless each is vividly visualized and conveyed with absolute sincerity—not merely assumed—your interpretation will be false, and therefore ridiculous. To overdo the emotion is even worse than not to realize it sufficiently, because it shows a lack of restraint and balance and is an insult to intelligence. Restraint and balance are things you must cultivate, and in doing so you will develop your critical faculty and discipline your imagination. Try it. It is the finest discipline in the world, because it is not superimposed, which would be a cramping of your being, but it is a way of growing and becoming more yourself.

25. "ng" as in "ring".

ŋ
"NG"

Symbol: ENG
Phonemic classification: lingua-velar voiced nasal
IPA usage: "ring"; "bank"; "running"
American English usage: same as IPA.

This consonant is made by allowing the sound to flow through the nose while the base of the tongue is in contact with the soft palate.

It is a nasal consonant like "m" and "n". It is known as a liquid consonant because it can be sustained and because it has great vocality. Other liquid consonants are: "l", "m", "n", "ng" and "r".

"ng" is a very good consonant to use for the improvement of head resonance.

a. Make a list of words containing this consonant, e.g., ringing, singing, swinging, bringing.

b. Make up some verses that will afford you practice in saying this sound so that at any future date you will not be tempted to drop the "g" in "ng", e.g.:

A sparrow sat on a steeple,
And listened to a bell,
"I'll fly down to the people
And then," he said, "I'll tell
Them what the bell is ringing
When it calls aloud,
  DING DONG,
It's singing,
  singing,
    singing,
Aloud its favourite song."

"Oh, come along: oh, come along,
  Oh, come along, you people,
And listen to me ringing,
  ringing,
    ringing,
From the steeple.

I crash, and boom and echo,
A sombre, mournful, song—
So listen, very carefully,
  Ding-dong,
    Ding-dong,
      DING-DONG!"

—*D.L.*

c. The following verses will give you practice in saying the sound "ng".

Selection from the Pied Piper

Into the street the Piper stept,
Smiling first a little smile,
As if he knew what magic slept
In his quiet pipe the while:
Then like a musical adept,
To blow his pipe his lips he wrinkled,
And green and blue his sharp eyes twinkled,
Like a candle-flame where salt is sprinkled:
And ere three shrill notes the pipe uttered,
You heard as if an army muttered;
And the muttering grew to a grumbling,

And the grumbling to a mighty rumbling;
And out of the houses the rats came tumbling.
Great rats, small rats, lean rats, brawny rats,
Brown rats, black rats, grey rats, tawny rats,
Grave old plodders, gay young friskers,
Fathers, mothers, uncles, cousins,
Cocking tails and pricking whiskers,
Families by tens and dozens.
Brothers, sisters, husbands, wives,
Followed the Piper for their lives.

—*Robert Browning.*

d. The two poems below will give you more practice in saying the sound "ng". Finish it off well every time and notice the effect the poet achieves by the use of this sound. How would you describe it? Does it make any contributions to the "singing" qualities of the poems?

The Bells of Youth

The Bells of Youth are ringing through the gateway of the South,
The primrose and celandine are out.
Spring has risen with a shout, a wild rose in her mouth
And is singing, singing, singing through the world.

The Bells of Youth are ringing from the forest to the mountain,
From the meadow to the moorland, hark, their ringing!
Ten thousand, thousand flashing streams and fern dappled fountains
Are flinging wide the song of youth, and onward flowing, singing.

The Bells of Youth are ringing through the gateways of the south.
The bannerets of green are now unfurled.
Spring has risen with a laugh, a wild rose in her mouth,
And is singing, singing, singing through the world.

—*William Sharp.*

The Fifteen Acres

I cling and swing
On a branch, or sing
Through the cool, clear hush of morning, O:
Or fling my wing
On the air, and bring
To sleepier birds a warning; O:
That the night's in flight,
And the sun's in sight,

And the dew is the grass adorning, O:
And the green leaves swing
As I sing, sing, sing,
Up by the river,
Down the dell,
To the little wee nest,
Where the big tree fell,
So early in the morning, O.

I flit and twit,
In the sun for a bit
When his light so bright is shining, O:
Or sit and fit
My plumes, or knit,
Straw plaits for the nest's nice lining, O:
And she with glee
Shows unto me
Underneath her wings reclining, O:
And I sing that Peg
Has an egg, egg, egg,
Up by the oat-field,
Round the mill
Past the meadow
Down the hill,
So early in the morning, O.

I stoop and swoop
On the air, or loop
Through the trees, and then go soaring, O:
To group with a troop
On the gusty poop
While the wind behind is roaring, O:
I skim and swim
By a cloud's red rim
And up to the azure floorings, O:
And my wind wings drip
As I slip, slip, slip
Down through the rain-drops,
Back where Peg
Broods in the nest
On the little white egg,
So early in the morning, O.

—*James Stephens.*

Both of the previous poems are suitable for Choral Verse Speaking, which is not only a very useful way of obtaining practice in speech training, but it can be a satisfying, creative activity, for choral verse makes many demands on speakers. If a choir is to achieve a lovely piece of work it must practice until it is a unit of thought and feeling, which is manifest in the pace, the emphasis, the arrangement of pauses, inflection and modulation. The members of the choir must be able to convey the meaning of what they are saying, with variety, forcefulness, and sensitiveness, and yet at the same time speak as a unified group.

A choir can be any size from four to four hundred. The bigger the choir the more difficult it is to get the perfect unity that is the first essential, for there are always people who will rely on the imagination, and even the memory of their neighbors to get them through; and it is more difficult in a large number to know who these are, but their presence will be manifest in "the dragging of the pace", and in the monotony of the interpretation.

Where every member of the choir, however, is pulling his or her weight, using his voice to convey ideas with the same sensitiveness and imagination as he would, were he alone, and yet co-operating with his neighbor in the interpretation, most interesting and satisfying results can be obtained.

The arrangement of a verse speaking choir must, of course, be dependent on the numbers in the choir. A crescent shape is probably better than straight lines, but it should not be a complete semi-circle. If there are more rows than one, then they will look better, and better results will be obtained if the rows are raised on steps, or platforms, so that each row is raised about a foot above the row in front of it.

Some conductors arrange their choirs in the shape of an arrow head, beginning with one person in front, three in the next row, five in the third row, and so on.

It increases tremendously the sense of "working in one" if the choir members stand shoulder to shoulder, rather than if they are in scattered groups. Very pleasing and interesting effects can be obtained by grouping voices as dark, medium and light, and arranging these so that the dark-voiced group stands on one side of the medium-toned groups, and the lighter-voiced group on the other; but we do not make a space between each group. Let them still work as a unit.

A choir can be conducted or unconducted in the final performance. There should always be in the choir someone who can be relied on to lead the choir, so that the attack is never feeble or uncertain, and the pace reflects the meaning.

In schools most interesting work is often achieved by allowing one of the members of the class to conduct the choir, and at all times the co-operation of the whole choir should be invited, and all suggestions from choir members should be tried out—for two reasons. It is stimulating to have many minds working on a problem of interpretation, and sometimes surprising and original ideas emerge which enhance the beauty of the interpretation, but even when the suggestions cannot ultimately be used, trying them out quickens the critical faculty of the whole group, and trains the ear to perceive to what extent sound can re-echo sense.

In choral verse speaking, as in all other speaking, the sense matters above all things, and though originality in achieving effects is a desirable thing, the effects should never be merely ornamental or decorative, because then the artificiality will rob the performance of sincerity. All effects should be functional. They should make clearer the meaning and more powerful the impact of the poem on the mind and imagination of the listeners.

Certain forms of poetry lend themselves to choral verse speaking, while others do not. For instance, sonnets are usually poems which lend themselves better to interpretation by one person than by a group, but that does not mean that no lyrics are suitable. Avoid, in lyrics, however, a poem which expresses a highly individual mood as, for instance, Wordsworth's Sonnet *On Westminster Bridge*. On the other hand, do not choose poems in which there is great monotony of rhythm, even though it may be suitable matter for group speaking.

Choose poems in which the word pictures are vivid and there is opportunity for conveying an impression of strongly contrasted situations or ideas and feelings, as, for instance, in *Tarantella*. See Page 140.

All three poems given as exercises in saying "ng" are suitable for choral verse speaking.

26. "h" as in <u>h</u>orse.

h	
"h"	**Symbol:** LOWER-CASE H **Phonemic classification:** Glottal voiceless fricative **IPA usage:** "<u>h</u>orse"; "<u>h</u>uge" **American English usage:** same as IPA.

This sound is sometimes described as a forcible expulsion of breath. It is produced by a slight friction of breath between the vocal chords. In shaping it do not forget the importance of good breath control. Keep the chest raised—the ribs out—and remember to use the abdominal press. Breathe out audibly.

a. Exercises:

h h h	h h h	h h h	h
ho ho ho	ho ho ho	ho ho ho	ho
he he he	he he he	he he he	he
ha ha ha	ha ha ha	ha ha ha	ha
haw haw haw	haw haw haw	haw haw haw	haw
how how how	how how how	how how how	how
hoo hoo hoo	hoo hoo hoo	hoo hoo hoo	hoo
hay hay hay	hay hay hay	hay hay hay	hay

b. Make a list of fifty words which have the initial "h" sound, e.g., horse, hand, hose, herb, hide, huge, house, heavy, heat, however, happen, hoist.
c. Use some of these in nonsense rhymes which will afford further practice:

Hecuba Herbaceous

Hecuba Herbaceous
Was a heifer,
What a heifer,
Was the heifer
christened Hecuba Herbaceous!

"I might have been ham,"
  she thought,
"and smoked, and hung on hooks,"
  she thought,
"I'm really very glad I am a heifer,
  not a ham!
 and then
A Hippopotamus,
I really would have made a fuss,
To have a horrid figure,
 even bigger than a bus—
  SO
I'm glad I am a heifer,
 not a hippopotamus!"

And so she reasoned thus—
 "Horrid! Hippopotamus:
 Hateful,
  hanging, smoky Ham,
 How fortunate I am
That Hecuba Herbaceous,
a charming little Heifer,
Hecuba Herbaceous,
 quite as pretty as can be—
I'm really very happy,
 that she's no one else but ME!"

—*D.L.*

c. Be careful not to preface with the "h" sound words which begin with a vowel sound: eight, *not* (h)eight; am, *not* (h)am; ox, *not* (h)ox.
d. Make lists of words which will afford you practice in distinguishing the positions in which "h" should be heard:

ham .... am
hate .... eight
heat .... eat
hew .... ewe
howl .... owl

People who fall into the temptation of using an intrusive "h" before vowel sounds should slow down their speech. Visualize the spelling of the word, and consciously shape the vowel sound, at the beginning of the word, and then utter the word. In time a habit will develop and this difficulty will be overcome. People who have difficulty in controlling this sound usually have a rigid lower jaw. Learn to relax the lower jaw and at the same time keep the ribs extended so that no breath escapes without being vocalised.

e. *The dropped "h"*. Some people make the mistake of forgetting to say the "h" sound before the semi-vowel "y" [j]. These people say: yuge for huge, yuman for human, yue for hue.

Practice the following exercise:

Hi—y—oo	Hi—y—oo	Hi—y—oo
H—yoo	H—yoo	H—yoo

f. A common mistake nowadays is to fail to articulate the "h" in the following positions:
h ospital, h uge.

Many people fail to articulate "h" in combination with initial "w", as in when, which, whine. Practice the following sentence:

"Which witch whistled and which witch whined, when she saw the wine?"

Make up your own nonsense verse to afford you further practice in distinguishing between the articulating of [w] and [ʍ] (wh).

g. Say the following poem aloud, so often that you know it by heart:

An Old Woman of the Roads

O, to have a little house;
To own the hearth and stool and all,
The heaped up sods upon the fire,
The pile of turf against the wall!

To have a clock with weights and chains,
And pendulum swinging up and down;
A dresser filled with shining delf,
Speckled and white and blue and brown.

I could be busy all the day,
Clearing and sweeping hearth and floor;
And fixing on the shelf again
My white, and blue, and speckled store!

I could be quiet there at night
Beside the fire and by myself,
Sure of a bed, and loath to leave
The ticking clock and shining delf!

Och! but I'm weary of mist and dark.
And roads where there's never a house or bush.
And tired I am of bog and road,
And the crying wind and the lonesome hush.

And I'm praying to God on high,
And I'm praying Him night and day
For a little house . . . a house of my own,
Out of the wind and the rain's way.

—*Padraic Colum.*

In *An Old Woman of the Roads* is expressed the point of view, and the outlook, and the longings of an old woman. Not any or every old woman, but a particular one.

In what country would you expect to find her? Choose phrases from the poem that justify your opinion.

What are the circumstances of her life? What is her conception of happiness? What is your conception of happiness? Could you express it in verse? You might try.

Try to imagine the circumstances and the point of view of any person other than yourself, then try to communicate an impression of that person to your listener.

Notice the simplicity of the expression of ideas in this poem. In a poem of about 170 words there are only 22 words of more than one syllable. Is it in keeping with the character of the old woman that she should express herself in this fashion? How would you describe the language of this poem? If you cannot, find a word or two from the following list:

homely	polished	smooth
crude	rough	elegant
neat	simple	subtle

If you were asked to describe the atmosphere of this poem which word or words would you use from the following list:

pathetic	boisterous	desolate
melancholy	vigorous	dreary
wistful	cheerful	doleful

Chapter 8

The Art of Reading

Advice to those who wish to read well.

1. *Stand properly.*

   Hold your book in one hand, leaving the other free to turn the pages. Hold your book on eye level, but a little to the side, so that your face is not screened. The listener should be able to see your face.

2. *Be audible.*

   The first essential is to be heard. This is a matter of (*a*) breath control; (*b*) resonance; (*c*) enunciation.

3. *Be distinct.*

   This depends on the neatness and firmness of the contacts in shaping consonants.

4. *Be intelligible.*

   Remember that the sole justification for speaking is that you have something to say. If it does not make sense it should not be said. To read well is an even more difficult task than to speak well, because the reader has to interpret the words on the page so that he can convey, as though they were being spoken for the first time, the thoughts recorded on the page by means of groups of symbols called printed words.

   To convey meaning you must be able to use properly:

i. Phrasing.	iv. Inflection.
ii. Pause.	v. Variety.
iii. Emphasis.	vi. Pitch.

5. *Convey the feelings expressed as well as the thought.*

6. *Use your imagination all the time.*

   The test of a good reader is that he can make contact with the minds of his listeners and hold their attention because he is making them see the pictures and ideas, and feel the emotions recorded on the printed page. He should sound not as though he were reading but as though he were speaking without a book.

   This is a skill which requires years of training in the art of allowing the eye to move ahead of the words actually being spoken, so that the reader, knowing what is to come, may be able to make an efficient use of the technical devices for conveying meaning, namely, phrasing, pitch, pace and emphasis, inflection, pause.

The power to be able to read at sight is one of the final tests of a thoroughly trained speaker. It is not a gift. It is a power that is within the reach of all who have the honesty to gain a knowledge of how it is done, and the patience and sincerity to put into practice what they know. "Bookish theoric" is useless unless it is translated into action.

CHAPTER 9

The Art of Public Speaking

Never stand up in public to speak unless you have something worth saying. It is impolite to dare to waste people's time. To be a perfect public speaker you must learn to think from the point of view of your audience. Why are the people there? If you were in the audience what are the questions you would hope to hear the speaker answer?

When you are preparing your speech ask these questions and answer them in a logical sequence, 1, 2, 3, 4, 5, 6, etc.

This does *not* mean write out and memorize your speech. That is the worst possible thing to do, for if you are in a nervous state you may actually forget the words of your speech, and then you will be in a panic! It is far better to *memorize*, in sequence, the *points* you wish to make, or the questions you wish to answer, and then to practice answering them as though you were replying, in conversation, to someone.

Here is an example of how you should practice. Supposing you are asked to make a presentation of a gift, for which many people have subscribed, to a person who is leaving the firm, or the school, or the tennis or golf club, or a society. How would you set about it?

You would say: There are five points to remember if this speech is to be well done. Here are the five points in the right order:

1. *Introduce yourself.* Why have you been asked to make the presentation? Is it because you are (*a*) the director, (*b*) chairman, (*c*) oldest member?

   Whatever the reason, say how it is that the privilege of making the presentation falls to you.
2. *Introduce the recipient*, who is leaving, and say what his services have been.
3. *Give the reason why he is leaving*. It may be ill-health, or a transfer, marriage, or retirement. Every occasion differs in its details. See that what you say is relevant to the occasion.
4. *Say something about the gift.* Many people who have subscribed may not have seen it. If it is an appropriate gift, e.g., a clock for an unpunctual person, or even for a punctual person, it may furnish the opportunity for humour. Think of a gift when you are practicing your speech and visualize the whole situation clearly.
5. *Express* on behalf of the assembled company their *good wishes* towards their departing colleague, and the hope they will see him again at some future date.

If you can remember this framework, you will, in time, by dint of much practice, become expert in this type of speech. Always try to visualize the whole situation. Then you will be able to talk well.

Proceed to make a reply to the speech of presentation. You will find that this speech, too, can be organized round five points.

Think these out. They are very similar to the five points of the first speech:

1. Thank the speaker for what he has said about you.
2. Say something about your association with the organization.
3. Say something about your departure and express your regret at severing your connection with these people.
4. Say something about the gift.
5. Thank them for the gift and their good wishes, and possibly express the hope that you will at a future date meet them again.

Half the battle is won in public speaking if you know what you are going to say. The other half depends on how you say it.

Nervousness is a great handicap in public speaking. There are very few people who at all times feel completely confident.

It helps to allay nervousness and to give a speaker confidence if he knows:

1. That he has a clear grasp of his subject.
2. That he is free from speech defects of any kind. That means he must be audible, distinct, and technically equipped to express meaning, which means that he can make appropriate use of pace, pitch, pause, inflection, modulation and emphasis, with all of which this book has been concerned to give him some guidance.

Remember to establish a contact with your audience. Speak *to* them. Do not recite *at* them. They are there to give you a hearing, or obviously they would not have come. Do not embarrass them by showing how unhappy you feel in your situation. Enjoy yourself and they will also. Forget about your physical being, and concentrate on communicating the ideas you have come to express.

Successful Speaking

1. Your success as a Speaker depends both on technical and artistic factors.

Technical Skills:	Stance, Breathing, Voice Production, Enunciation, Articulation Pronunciation, Audibility and Distinctness.
Artistry:	Visualization, Creative imagination, Grasp of Meaning, Sensitivity, Audience Contact, Perceptivity, Sincerity, and Impact.

2. Adhere strictly to the time allocated to you as the Speaker. Do not exceed it.

3. STANCE:

   Stand in a balanced position, feet slightly apart.

   Weight equally distributed.

   Shifting of weight, unnecessary movement of the legs and "swaying in the breeze" are all movements which are distracting and should be avoided.

   Eyes on eye level. Do not lift your chin. Chest raised. Shoulders down.

4. AUDIBILITY:

   Depends on breath control and shaping vowel sounds in the oral cavity.

   Breathe in, extending the rib-cage laterally, and lifting the breastbone.

   Abdominal walls flat, no bulging.

   Exhale through a well opened mouth which means a relaxed lower jaw.

   Slightly contract the abdominal muscles so that the diaphragm slowly resumes its dome-shaped position, and the pressure on the vibrating column of breath is at the base of the lungs as the diaphragm returns to its convex position.

5. DISTINCTNESS:

   At all times speech must be distinct so that your listener is not under strain trying to make out the words you, the Speaker, are shaping.

   Finish final consonants firmly and crisply.

   Take time to make sure you are not slurring one word on to the next.

   Speak on your natural pitch.

   Do not strain your voice by speaking above your natural pitch. i.e. do not shout or scream.

   A strained voice prevents success in communication with your listener, because you communicate your strain to the listener.

6. PACE:

   The Speaker should adopt a suitable pace for his/her delivery. Do not rattle off your speech with little attention to the meaning which depends on correct Phrasing and use of Pause.

   The natural register of the voice is distorted by an incorrect pace.

   Never raise your voice. Shouting does not make you more easily heard.

   Speak on your natural register then you will not subject your listeners to tension or strain.

7. CUE CARDS:

   Cue cards can be tolerated if well handled. Each card should contain only one idea.

8. IMPACT OF PRESENTATION:

   Do not stand rigidly. Movement and gesture enhance the delivery, but such movements and gestures must not be superimposed or mechanical, they must be the natural, organic, spontaneous gestures and movements that are relevant to the meaning, and to the interpretation as you understand these.

9. INTERPRETATION:

   Words make pictures in your mind. See those pictures clearly in your mind or your listener cannot see them. Then He/She becomes bored because what is being said has no meaning. Remember that words carry not only the picture in your mind but how you feel about that picture. Learn to recognize your emotional response and express it truthfully though without exaggeration, or any form of exhibitism.

   Enjoy presenting your Speech. Then the listener will enjoy hearing it.

10. VISUAL IMPACT:

    The Speaker should be well groomed. It is a sign of self respect as well as respect for your listeners. Do not shamble in or look embarrassed.

    Speakers must assume their position on stage with quiet confidence and precision. First impressions count. Remember that you are the host and the members of the audience are your guests.

    Do not race off the stage after the last word has been spoken.

    Remain on stage for a few seconds for the presentation to sink in.

    Do not create the impression that you cannot wait to get off stage.

11. CONTACT:

    It is essential that the Speaker is able to include his/her audience in this act of Communication. By addressing the back row of the audience the speaker will be encouraged to have sufficient volume to be heard. The speaker should not talk at their audience but rather to them, as one human being to another.

    Focus on your listeners who are your guests who pay you the compliment of being willing to listen to you.

TECHNICAL FACTORS AND PRESENTATION:

12. Quotes: A very ugly but commonly used gesture i.e. the wiggling of the fingers of both hands to indicate inverted commas, is not permitted in Public Speaking. Speakers should be able to use vocal inflection to indicate to their audiences that what follows is a quote. Beware of using too much of an authority's own speech where there is a need to read what is to be conveyed. The information should rather be paraphrased and presented in the Speaker's own words.
13. Definition of theme and logical sequence in the development of ideas in the presentation thereof is essential if you are to win the respect of your listeners.
14. Accurate use of vocabulary is a sign of intelligence and awareness.

15. Freedom from strain. You can only be relaxed if you have the confidence borne of an adequate amount of rehearsal over the preceding months.
16. Sincerity.
17. Power to include the listeners in this act of Communication.

    Do not focus on yourself but on your listeners.
18. Remember, when you are speaking in Public, that you are representative of your parents, your school, and your community, so do them the courtesy of being well prepared.
19. A Speaker should not read from notes. He should remember that he is making a speech not delivering a Paper.
20. Be prepared well in advance so that you speak with ease, and enjoyment.

Summary of Points to Remember

1. Never allow your Speech to exceed the time allocated to you. If the allowance of time for your speech is ten minutes don't exceed that time by speaking for another thirty minutes!
2. A good speaker arranges the ideas in his speech in a logical order. These different examples are given:

A Speech Presentation

STRUCTURE:

1. Introduce yourself.
2. Introduce the recipient.
3. What is the occasion?
4. What is the presentation?
5. Express the good wishes of the assembled group.

HINTS:

1. A good speaker answers all the questions that arise spontaneously in the mind of the listener.
2. Never memorize the words of the speech. Memorize the five ideas. Do not memorize the words you intend to use your in your speech. Practice daily, saying your speech aloud. You will be surprise at how many different ways you can express yourself. These will increase every time you practice.
3. Do not be satisfied with rough work. Polish to perfection every sentence you utter.
4. Recreate the total situation vividly as though you were speaking to a blind person. Create the total milieu as you speak. Remember that you are representing not merely yourself, but a great number of people who wish to express their good will towards, and their appreciation of the person to whom the gift is being given.

A Speech of Thanks Made by the Recipient of a Gift

STRUCTURE:

1. Introduce yourself.
2. Introduce the presenter.
3. Introduce the occasion.
4. Introduce the gift.
5. Express the appreciation of your colleagues/workers/whatever.

HINTS:

1. Never memorize the words of your speech. Memorize the points on which the speech is based.
2. Remember, that in public, you never speak for yourself alone. You represent your school, your club, your organization, the whole background from which you have emerged.
3. Practice every day! Perfect every detail and polish every sentence so that a better choice of words or a more pleasing way of expressing the same idea may come into your mind.

A Report

STRUCTURE:

The five points with which you have become familiar in the two previous types of speech are the same for a Report. The embellishments will be your own as you create the situation in which the Report will be delivered orally.

Namely:

1. Introduce yourself.
2. Welcome the audience.
3. Make apologies if necessary.
4. Introduce the report on the project you have chosen to research.
5. Recapitulate the most memorable points made in your report. Then state your recommendations clearly. In closing, throw the subject open to the audience for questions and comments.

CHAPTER 10

Conclusion

The foregoing chapters do not pretend to furnish an exhaustive treatise on good speech. There is much more to be known about speech sounds, about verse-speaking, choral verse, drama, and public speaking. The mere fringe of these subjects has been touched with a view to stimulating the interest of the ordinary person in a field of study and achievement which alone can assure his full development as a civilized human being.

In this book only the barest outline has been given in an attempt to indicate how this study may profitably be pursued. There is much more to know about every aspect of the subject which covers a vast field, including speech deviations on the one hand and, on the other, drama and poetry, which are the highest artistic achievements of speech, for you must realize that a poet or dramatist is not only a skilled craftsman handling the tool of speech, but a person whose skill transcends that of even a master craftsman, so that he feels impelled to make the instrument that he uses completely expressive of his vision of life.

'Speech is to thought what protoplasm is to life,' says Julian Huxley, and if that is true, speech is the basis of civilization, for nothing that man has accomplished but first existed as a thought. All man ever does is to externalize, in brick and mortar, in iron and steel, in organization and institution, in human relationships and in action, his thoughts, however adequate, or limited, these may be. That they are too limited in many cases, all will readily agree. Therefore it behoves us to train and develop his power of thought and feeling to the point of integration which gives him the developed imagination without which he can never fully realize his world.

The speech work selected in that process of education must keep pace with the growing ability of the human being to control this instrument for communicating ideas, until, at length, he is able to unravel complex ideas and complex feelings, as they are expressed in great poetry, and especially great dramatic poetry where the infinite variety of human complexity in thought and response is to be found mirrored. But we shall never be able to do it unless we take to heart the lesson Hamlet illustrated with the recorders, for the benefit of Rosencrantz and Guildenstern:

Hamlet: *Will you play upon this pipe.*
Guil: *My lord, I cannot.*
Hamlet: *I pray you.*
Guil: *Believe me, I cannot.*
Hamlet: *I do beseech you.*

Guil: *I know no touch of it, my lord.*

Hamlet: *Tis as easy as lying; govern these vantages with your finger and thumb, give it breath with your mouth, and it will discourse most eloquent music. Look you, these are the stops.*

Guil: *But these cannot I command to my utterance of harmony; I have not the skill.*

Hamlet: *Why, look you now, how unworthy a thing you make of my stops; you would pluck out the heart of my mystery; you would sound me from my lowest note to the top of my compass; and there is much music, excellent voice, in this little organ, yet cannot you make it speak. 'Sblood, do you think I am easier to be played on than a pipe? Call me what instrument you will, though you can fret me, you cannot play upon me.*

If you would make speech the instrument of communication—and great literature is after all 'memorable speech'—you must learn its possibilities, you must know its 'stops', and be able to sound it from the lowest note to the top of its compass, if you would 'pluck out the heart of its mystery', and until you humbly submit yourself to this discipline, 'though you may fret, you cannot play'. But take heart, it is no mystery, no rare gift. It is the privilege of all who are honest enough to seek knowledge and understanding, and have the patience to put into practice what they know and understand.

INDEX

JINGLES

CONSONANTS

VOWELS

POEMS

PROSE

AUTHORS

Verse

PROSE